Rembrandt Drawings

Bob Haak

Rembrandt
Drawings

T & H

Thames and Hudson · London

Illustration on front: *Sleeping Girl* (see plate 85)

Translated by Elizabeth Willems-Treeman

© 1974 Verlag M. DuMont Schauberg, Cologne

First published by Thames and Hudson, 1976

Printed and bound in Italy by Garzanti Editore, Milan

Contents

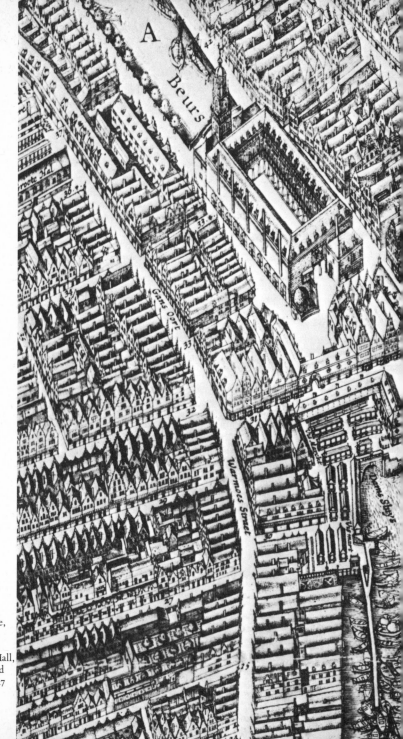

B. F. van Berckenrode,
Detail of his map of
Amsterdam, with the
Dam, the old Town Hall,
the Weigh-House, and
the Nieuwe Kerk, 1647

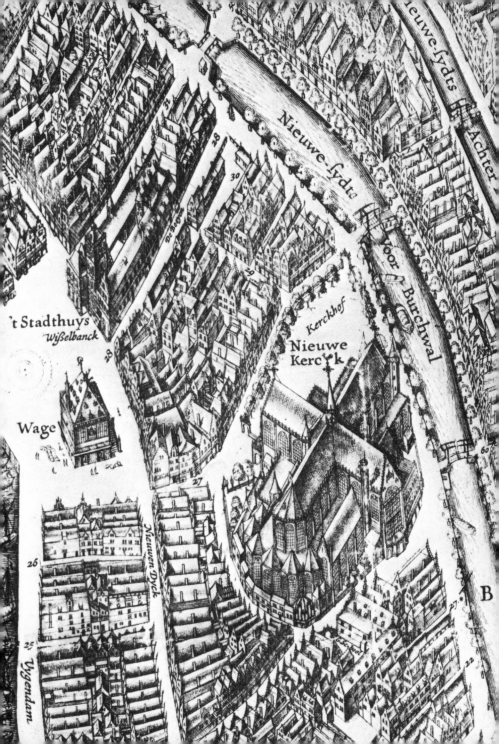

Nieuwe-ſydts

Nieuwe-ſydts

Achter

Nieuwe-ſydta

28

30

de hof

Voor

29

Burchwal

Kerchhof

't Stadthuys

Wiſſelbanck

Nieuwe
Kerck

28

60

Wage

27

26

Nieuwen Dyck

B

27

25

22

Vygendam

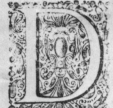

DE Curateur over den Insol=
venten Boedel van Reinbrant van Rijn / konstigh
Schilder / sal / als by de E. E Heeren Commissari=
sen der Desolate Boedelen hier ter Stede daer toe ge=
authoriseert / by Executie verkopen de vordere Papier
Kunst onder den selven Boedel als noch berustende/
bestaende inde Konst van verscheyden der voornaemste so Italiaensche/
Fransche/ Duytsche ende Nederlandtsche Meesters / ende by den selven
Rembrant van Rijn met een groote curieashyt te samen versamelt.

Gelijck dan mede een goede partye van
Teeckeningen ende Schetsen vanden selven Rembrant van Rijn selven

De verkopinge sal wesen ten daeghe/
ure ende Jaere als boven / ten huyse van
Barent Jansz Schuurman / Waert in
de Keysers Kroon / inde Kalver straet/
daer de verkopinge voor desen is geweest,

Segget voort,

"A goodly parcel of Drawings and Sketches by the same Rembrant van Rijn himself"

When, in 1656, Rembrandt at his own request was declared insolvent because he could no longer pay his debts, his possessions – except what he needed for his personal maintenance – had to be sold to satisfy the claims of his creditors. A list of his movable property was drawn up, and this inventory gives us an insight into his extensive art collection.[1] There are many indications that this collection was not exclusively a private one but had been partly assembled because Rembrandt was an active art dealer. At auction sales, he sometimes bought several specimens of the same print;[2] in his petition to the High Court for legal cession of estate, he pleaded "losses suffered in business" as the principal reason for his financial distress;[3] and, in the inventory, mention is made several times of paintings half-owned by another dealer. It is therefore difficult to determine which paintings and prints belonged to Rembrandt's own collection and which must be considered as part of the art dealing. Perhaps the dividing line was also never very clear to Rembrandt himself.

The number of prints and drawings he possessed was so large that a special auction of "Paper Art" was held in the autumn of 1658 at the inn De Keizerskroon in the Kalverstraat, Amsterdam. The announcement of this sale has been preserved (see page 8); in it, besides the work of the "most eminent Italian/French/German and Netherlandish Masters/and gathered together by the same Rembrant van Rijn with a great curiosity," special notice is given of "A goodly parcel of Drawings and Sketches by the same Rembrant van Rijn himself."

Rembrandt's extreme interest in and love for drawing and the graphic arts is evident from the inventory. We shall here pay particular attention to his own work and not to the rest of the collection, which included many artists – such "classics" as Mantegna, Dürer, Lucas van Leiden, and Maarten van Heemskerck, and such contemporaries as Bloemaert, Lastman, Buytewech, Jordaens, and Rubens.

Collectors in Rembrandt's day, and long thereafter, had the excellent custom of keeping drawings in "art books," often handsomely bound albums with blank pages, between which the individual drawings were laid. These albums were kept in a cabinet especially designed to hold them. In Rembrandt's inventory, his own drawings are listed as follows:

One large book, full of sketches by Rembrant (2 x)
One book bound in black leather with the best sketches by Rembrant
One book, full of drawings made by Rembrant, consisting of men and women, nude
One ditto full of landscapes, drawn from life by Rembrant
One packet full of antique drawings by Rembrant
5 little books in quarto, full of drawings by Rembrant
One parchment book full of landscapes after life by Rembrant
One ditto full of figure sketches by Rembrant (2 x)
One little book full of faces drawn by Rembrant
One ditto full of Statues by Rembrant drawn from life (2 x)
One ditto sketches by Rembrant drawn with the pen (5 x)
One ditto quarto full of sketches by Rembrant
Several packets with sketches by Rembrant and others

From this listing it appears that at least eight art albums, more than ten little "boekiens," which perhaps were sketchbooks, and a number of packets of drawings were present in Rembrandt's studio. It is difficult to estimate just how many sheets there were in the whole collection. Of the two small albums of "Statues," only a few sheets are now known (one is reproduced as plate 32); by analogy, one is inclined to think, only a fraction of all the drawings can have been preserved. The chances of survival, however, were probably much greater for drawings whose subject matter was considered more important. For Rembrandt always had an excellent reputation as draftsman, and collectors through the centuries have highly valued his drawings. In 1680 the estate of the sea painter Jan van de Capelle, an admirer of the master's work, included five portfolios with drawings by Rembrandt – approximately five hundred sheets in all. These most likely derived from the auction sale in 1658. Rembrandt no doubt had well over a thousand, if not several thousand, drawings in his studio at the time the inventory was made.

What happened to all these drawings? How many have survived? In the case of only one fairly large group, still intact, do we know the history. Each of the landscapes in the beautiful series in the Chatsworth Settlement collection is marked with an F and was purchased by the second Duke of Devonshire in 1723 from Nicolaas Flinck, son of Rembrandt's pupil Govert Flinck (plates 57, 59, 60).

It is obvious that we are here confronted with one of the albums "full of landscapes after life," or with a portion of the drawings from such a book.

For the rest, however, the drawings are scattered all over the world, and no one will ever discover how many of the "goodly parcel" of 1658 or of the drawings that Rembrandt subsequently made have been lost. The most recent oeuvre catalogue lists approximately fourteen hundred of Rembrandt's drawings.[4]

Authenticity and Dating

It might be supposed that the authenticity of Rembrandt's drawings poses no particular problem. A drawing, more than a painting, is generally thought to be a direct and spontaneous expression of an artist's personality and talent. On closer scrutiny, however, this hypothesis does not hold up, or perhaps it would be more accurate to say that our powers of discrimination and judgment are not sufficient to ensure our infallibility in determining the characteristics of a draftsman's handwriting. It is indeed not always possible to distinguish Rembrandt's hand from those of his most gifted pupils or even from later imitators.

In the training that Rembrandt gave his pupils – and he taught throughout his entire career, from 1628 onward – drawing was of great importance, as was customary in the seventeenth century. Before the pupil was allowed to begin painting, he had first to qualify in drawing, which included making copies after his own and other masters. Samuel van Hoogstraten, who studied under Rembrandt from about 1640 to 1648, published a book called *Inleyding tot de Hooge Schoole der Schilderkonst* (Introduction to the Advanced Study of the Art of Painting) in 1678. In it he wrote: "Usually the pupils are set to copying eyes, noses, mouths, ears, and various faces, and further, prints of all sorts.... In order to learn a good method, it is of great advantage to copy extremely fine drawings very early; for thus does one find in a short time what another long sought for."

A fairly large number of copies by pupils of Rembrandt's drawings can be identified today. As long as the original still exists, the copy can be distinguished from it without too much difficulty, no matter how skillful the pupil was. But if the original is lost, the complications multiply. A number of drawings once thought to be by Rembrandt have later, when better versions appeared, had to be removed from his oeuvre.

It is perhaps also characteristic of Rembrandt's strong personality that, under his direct supervision and leadership, his pupils followed his style as exactly as possible and seemed capable of better performances than when they were afterwards on their own. Moreover, we must always keep in mind that Rembrandt corrected the work of his pupils. A drawing by Constant van Renesse, reproduced below, may well be an example of this: the angel as initially drawn has clearly been corrected by someone else, presumably Rembrandt.

Finally, the forgers. It must be admitted that some of them have been so clever that they lead art historians astray. Rembrandt himself played into their hands, for he signed far too few of his drawings.

All this makes it sometimes extraordinarily difficult to attribute a drawing to Rembrandt with any certainty, and it is therefore not surprising that the various experts often do not agree. Differences of opinion regarding the dating of the sheets also occur. Dated drawings are even rarer than signed ones, and although

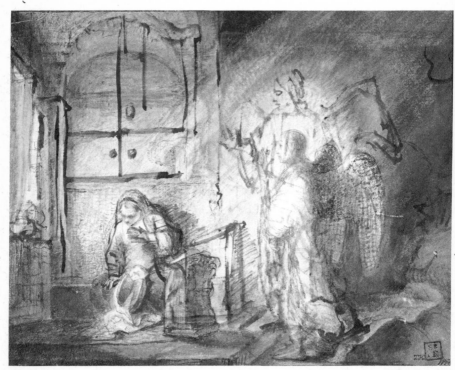

Constant van Renesse, corrected by Rembrandt, *The Annunciation.* Pen and brush, brown and gray ink, red chalk, 173 x 231 mm. Kupferstichkabinett, Staatliche Museen, Berlin-Dahlem

it is possible to trace a general line of development, we must never forget that the circumstances under which and the purpose for which a drawing was made may have been of great influence on the execution. Presumably associated paintings or etchings form merely imperfect clues. Only in those cases in which a direct and clear relationship and link between an undated drawing and a dated painting or etching can be established – as, for example, with the *Judas Returning the Thirty Pieces of Silver* (plates 4, 4a) and the portraits of Anslo (plates 31, 31a) and Sylvius (plates 45, 45a) – is it possible to date the drawing with any accuracy. In other instances, a drawing which Rembrandt assimilated into a painted or etched composition may have originated earlier, perhaps much earlier. The presence of so many drawings in his studio is indeed evidence that he kept these sheets handy for reference and use whenever he needed them.

Even when a painted composition seems based on a preparatory drawing by Rembrandt, one must be extremely cautious in concluding that the painting is also by him, for there is little doubt that Rembrandt's pupils followed their master in working from his sketches. Such, I believe, was the situation with the painting *The Vision of the Prophet Daniel* (see page 15), executed by a pupil after a

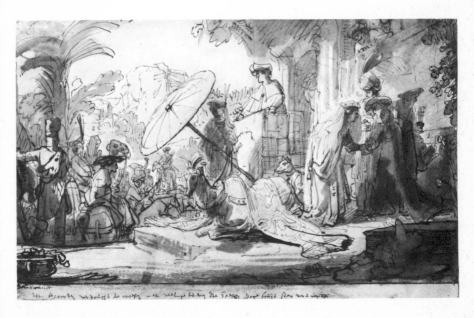

The Departure of Rebecca, c. 1637. Pen and brush, brown ink, 185 x 306 mm. Staatsgalerie, Stuttgart

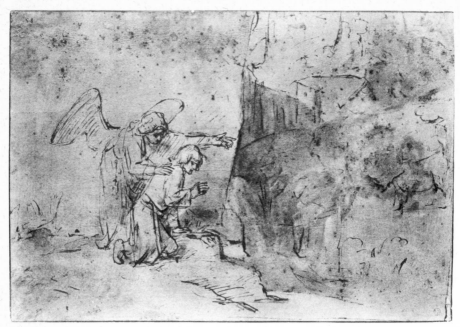

The Vision of the Prophet Daniel, c. 1650–55. Pen and brush, brown ink, heightened with white, 165 x 243 mm. Louvre, Paris

drawing by Rembrandt (see above). It is also likely that the line in Rembrandt's handwriting at the bottom of the drawing *The Departure of Rebecca* (see page 13) represents just such an instruction by the master to a pupil: "This should be amplified with many neighbors who watch this high[born] bride depart." By this he meant that the sketch should be worked out, presumably by a pupil, with more figures.

In regard to all this, we must constantly be aware that the training given by Rembrandt extended much further than the ordinary master-pupil relationship as set forth in the guild regulations, which were based on the customs of the craft guilds.[5] During the period of his greatest fame, Rembrandt regularly had at least twenty or more pupils, and his instruction of them can best be compared with that of an art academy attended not only by prospective young painters but also by amateurs who wished to draw from live models. A drawing by a pupil gives an impression of such a lesson (see page 16). A nude model is posing, and we can see that the pupils vary quite considerably in age. On the ledge above the model are plaster busts used for other drawing exercises.

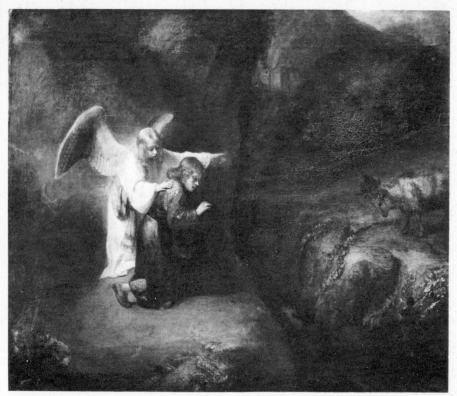

Pupil of Rembrandt (Barend Fabritius?), *The Vision of the Prophet Daniel*, c. 1650-55. Canvas, 96×116 cm. Gemäldegalerie, Staatliche Museen, Berlin-Dahlem

Sorts of Drawings

In the work of many artists, particularly the Italians, the various sorts of drawings can be clearly differentiated according to the purpose for which they were made: a sketch after a model done simply as a study; a first idea or a preparatory drawing for the composition of a painting; a definitive design or a *modello* executed to give the patron an idea of the artist's intentions; and, lastly, the drawing as a work of art in itself.

Although all these forms can be found among Rembrandt's drawings, the boundaries between them are extremely vague. Drawings as an end in themselves, as independent works of art, can rarely be pointed out with certainty. One such, however, is the 1634 portrait of a gentleman (plate 12), which qualifies for this category on grounds of technique and execution, choice of material and measurements. The portrait is, most exceptionally, drawn on vellum. The combination of red and black chalk with pen and ink was used but seldom by Rembrandt, and seldom did he, as here, fully sign and date a drawing. Perhaps he also originally meant for the large sheet *Christ Among His Disciples* of the same year (colorplate 2) to be an independent work. Format, technique, and signature would lead one to think so, but what about the corrections? Rembrandt drew one of the central figures on a separate piece of paper, which he then pasted in place. Presumably he did not intend to offer this sheet for sale.

It is uncertain whether Rembrandt ever drew a *modello* to show to a patron before he began a painting. The one drawing that might be so construed is the portrait of Maria Trip (plate 29), whom he painted in 1639 in somewhat modi-

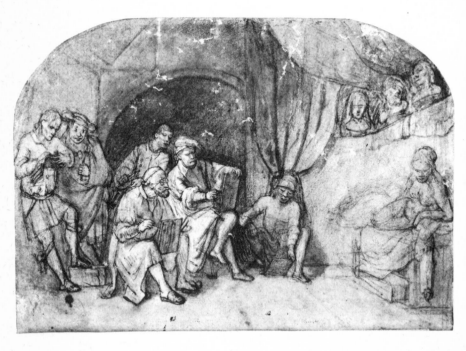

Pupil of Rembrandt, *Pupils in Rembrandt's Studio, Drawing from a Nude Model*, c. 1650-55. Pen and brush, brown ink, black chalk, heightened with white, 180 x 266 mm. Hessisches Landesmuseum, Darmstadt

fied form (plate 29a). The drawing is vigorous in design; at the same time, it has been worked out in a way – with both pen and brush in brown ink, touched with red chalk and heightened with white – that might be expected of a *modello*. A number of other portrait studies (plates 31 and 45, for example) must be considered as direct preliminary studies for an etching or a painting.

No worked-out preparatory studies for Rembrandt's history pieces are known to us; there are, however, a few rapid sketches that seem to anticipate a composition as a whole. The earliest example is the sketch for *Judas Returning the Thirty Pieces of Silver* (plate 4). Although considerable alterations are evident in the final composition (plate 4a), careful study of the painting and of X-ray photographs made of it reveals that Rembrandt's initial design for the painting closely followed the drawing: the silhouetted, back-turned figure in the foreground was originally given the same important compositional role in the painting that it had in the sketch. Rembrandt then abandoned his first idea and introduced drastic changes.

It is striking that no sketches have been preserved for such important commissions as *The Anatomy Lesson of Dr. Nicolaes Tulp* (1632) and *The Night Watch* (1642), for Rembrandt must have concentrated intensely on the composition of these works. A few drawings are known, however, for the three important official commissions of his later period. He made various studies of individual figures (see plate 93, for example) for *The Sampling Officials of the Drapers' Guild* (1662; plate 93a). Another sketch (plate 86) may be directly connected with *The Anatomy Lesson of Dr. Joan Deyman* (1656; plate 86a), but the purpose of this drawing is not entirely clear. The composition has been sketched very perfunctorily, yet around it can be seen not only the frame but also something of the surroundings – ceiling beams at the top and part of a shutter on the left side. Consequently, Van Regteren Altena has argued[6] that the sketch, once considered a preparatory study, more likely originated after the painting was finished, Rembrandt having drawn it to show the framing and placement of his large canvas in the chambers of the Surgeons' Guild. The small sketch (plate 91) for the painting *The Conspiracy of the Batavians* (1661-62; plate 91a), commissioned for the Amsterdam Town Hall, was also perhaps not a preliminary study but a suggestion of changes that Rembrandt wanted to make in the painting.[7]

There are certain drawings that might be interpreted as preparatory studies for a total composition, except for the fact that no direct connection with any painting can now be demonstrated. The great majority of these should probably be regarded as ideas that never got worked out. They indeed form the largest group of the extant drawings: fleeting notions, rapidly sketched impressions of events, actions, gestures, facial expressions. It is seldom possible to determine whether they were drawn from life or from the imagination. They are the true basis of Rembrandt's painted and etched work, yet rarely a direct preparation for it. Although we sometimes find a particular sketch worked into a painting or etching (see plates 25 and 25a, for example), it is impossible to decide whether it is a preliminary study or a drawing from life that Rembrandt subsequently adapted into a painted or etched composition.

Some drawings, of course, can immediately be recognized as studies from life: the many women with children (plates 14, 17, 18), the sheets on which the same figure is drawn in varying attitudes (plates 10, 19), the nude studies, the drawings of animals and landscapes. In a few instances we can discern that such a study changed function in a subsequent phase: a beggar (plate 3), which belongs to a series of figures that Rembrandt drew in black chalk in a sketchbook, reappears virtually unchanged in an etching, but there in the role of St. Peter (plate 3a).

Rembrandt also copied the work of other artists. It was customary in the seventeenth century to make use of examples of earlier or contemporary art. Not only the motif but also certain compositional solutions were taken over. The high demands which art critics of our day place upon originality did not then exist. The large collection in Rembrandt's studio of prints and drawings by other artists must therefore be considered in part as a source of inspiration, as a reservoir of working material.

From it Rembrandt chose to copy a print of Leonardo da Vinci's *The Last Supper* (plate 16). The composition must have appealed to him greatly, for he used the situation of many people around a table as early as 1638 in his painting of Simon's wedding feast (Bredius 507) and as late as 1661-62 in *The Conspiracy of the Batavians* (plate 91a). Rembrandt also made copies after Mantegna and after his own teacher, Pieter Lastman.

Particularly striking are his copies (plates 79, 80) after a series of Hindustan miniatures that derived from the court of the Mogul emperors who ruled over India in the seventeenth century. Rembrandt must have made at least twenty-five. That, in any event, was the number still together in one collection in 1747. About twenty survive today. In this instance, too, we see that Rembrandt not only copied the originals but used them in his own work as well. His etching *Abraham Entertaining the Angels* (Bartsch 29) is clearly based on the composition of one of the miniatures of which he also made a drawn copy (plates 79, 79a).

Subject Matter

Rembrandt himself classified his drawings primarily by subject matter – at least, as we saw in the inventory, the nude studies, the landscapes, the "antique drawings," the "Statues," and the figure sketches were stored in separate albums. Did he perhaps keep the "best sketches" apart in order to have them handy for sale? Just what the "antique drawings" comprised is not certain. Were they copies after the "classical" masters? Or was their subject matter based on ancient history? It is remarkable that the group forming by far the largest part of Rembrandt's oeuvre – the biblical subjects – cannot be distinguished as such in the inventory.

Rembrandt was first and foremost a history painter, that is to say, the most important things to him were the story itself and the rendering of its essence by means of human emotions expressed in face and gesture. The Bible was without doubt his major source of thematic material. Using the Old and the New Testaments and the Apocrypha as well, he painted, etched, and drew more "histories" than any other artist of his time. He had a clear preference for certain stories – that of Tobias, for example. And besides the biblical material, he used subjects from classical history and mythology.

It is important to realize, however, that he nearly always stuck to themes that had already been used by other artists. From this we can conclude – and comparison bears out this conclusion – that Rembrandt sought inspiration not so much from literature as from works of art, especially the graphic art of the fifteenth and sixteenth centuries.[8] Yet the impression remains that, particularly insofar as the Bible stories are concerned, he studied the writings and "lived" the story himself. In the last analysis, it is not so much the choice of subject matter that makes Rembrandt's art unique, but what he did with his material.

Still, it is hardly ever simple and sometimes not even possible to identify Rembrandt's subjects. For instance, does the old man in a chair, with a woman standing beside him (plate 37), represent a scene from daily life or, as has been suggested, either Abraham and Sarah or Jacob and Rachel listening to Joseph relating his dreams?

One of the albums owned by Jan van de Capelle contained one hundred and thirty-five drawings of "women at home with children." Some of these can still be identified, and they form a distinct part of Rembrandt's work – sketches he undoubtedly made directly from life, acute observations of a woman picking up a struggling child (plate 14), protectively shielding a child (who is wearing a "fall-down hat") from an over-friendly dog (plate 17), or tenderly carrying a child downstairs (plate 18). It is improbable that Rembrandt here depicted his own children. The first three of his and Saskia's babies – Rumbartus, the first Cornelia, and the second Cornelia – were born in 1635, 1638, and 1640, respectively, but none of them lived longer than a month or so. Titus, who did survive, was born in 1641. The drawings, on stylistic grounds, must be dated about 1636.

There is definitely a straightforward connection between Rembrandt's domestic life and the drawings of Saskia: her portrait (colorplate 1), and the more genre-like sketches of her looking out of a window (plate 11) and lying ill in bed (plate 30).

These homey little scenes especially appealed to Rembrandt in the years between 1635 and 1640 to 1642. Later he treated them much less frequently, and at the end of his life not at all. He was also fond of sketching himself now and then, at the beginning as an exercise, concentrating on facial expression and the fall of light (plate 1), later standing four-square, with his hands on his sides (plate 81) – a drawing impressive in its great simplicity.

Drawing from nude models was important to Rembrandt, as can be deduced from the album listed in the inventory as "full of drawings by Rembrant, consisting of men and women, nude." Several dozen of such drawings still exist, and it is noteworthy that Rembrandt continued until quite late in his career – into the 1660s – to draw from nude models (plate 87).

Traveling circuses were not uncommon in the seventeenth century, and we know from various sources that the residents of Amsterdam relished these entertainments, which gave them a chance to get acquainted with wild and foreign animals. Rembrandt must have shared in this delight, and lost no opportunity to draw the animals (plates 9, 21, 70). He was able to use the sketches he made of lions, in particular, in other works: the drawing *Daniel in the Lions' Den* (plate 71) and the painting *The Concord of the State* (1641; Bredius 476).

The landscape drawings comprise a separate chapter in Rembrandt's work. Though linked directly to the etched landscapes, they seem to have been little used for the painted ones, which, with a few exceptions, are fanciful idealizations, in character sometimes threatening, sometimes cosmic. The drawn landscapes, by contrast, were made straight from nature and with a marked propensity to simplification. Since Rembrandt was primarily a history and portrait painter who occasionally painted a landscape, he probably never pretended to specialize in the latter. History pieces were by far the most prestigious in his time, portraits the most financially profitable. That he nevertheless felt so strongly attracted to the drawing of landscapes – about two hundred and fifty of which have survived – can only indicate a pure aesthetic interest and sense of fulfillment, which existed more or less apart from his ambitions as a painter.

Rembrandt presumably drew his first landscapes in the mid-1630s, the last about 1655. In many instances the place where he made them can still be identified. He seems to have wandered about mainly in the neighborhood of Amsterdam, along the Amstel River and the wide IJ harbor,[9] but he also sometimes ventured further afield. A number of drawings of the little town of Rhenen on the Rhine River (colorplate 4, plate 48), in the southeast corner of Utrecht Province, bear witness to this.

In Amsterdam itself he drew rather little. He does not seem to have been very interested in the important buildings being erected or in the new canals and houses. He did make a drawing of the old Town Hall after it burned down in 1652 (plate 66), but he did not sketch the new one. When he drew the Montelbaanstoren (plate 67), he omitted the spire which had been added as ornament to this old fortress tower in 1606.

Material

Rembrandt's choice of material was relatively simple. Ordinarily he used white paper of small size, only now and then a larger sheet. He also worked in sketchbooks, presumably especially when he was drawing out-of-doors after nature. Sometimes he used paper of a brownish or yellowish tint; a few times he colored it himself before he began to draw. Vellum he saved for subjects worthy of it: the delicate little betrothal portrait of Saskia (colorplate 1), which he most exceptionally drew with silverpoint, and the portrait of a gentleman (plate 12), which must be considered an independent work of art. For his copies of the Hindustan miniatures, he chose Japanese paper with a silky sheen. He sometimes also used quite arbitrary pieces of paper, such as leaves from a cashbook (plate 93) or the reverse of a funeral announcement (plate 91).

Black and red chalk and pen and ink were by far his favorite mediums. The chalk drawings predominate in the early period, but later, after about 1650, very few of them appear. Rembrandt used pen and ink, however, all his life. The ink is usually brown bister or sepia, occasionally a darker East India ink. He used an opaque white for highlights or to make corrections.

Rembrandt drew with both goose-quill and reed pens. The quill is suppler and better suited for rapid, sensitive lines and the refining of details. The reed is tougher and can be employed for both sharp lines and broad, forceful strokes, according to how the pen is sharpened. Although the use of the quill or the reed cannot be linked to particular periods in Rembrandt's development, in general it may be said that he drew with the quill more often in his youth and with the reed in his maturity, when monumentality began to play a larger role in his work and the desire for detail diminished. He used a brush to wash a drawing, especially to indicate shadows, and to draw with as well. Several of his most beautiful sheets are drawn solely with the brush (plate 85).

Development

Rembrandt's development as painter and etcher can be followed without much trouble. He dated many of his paintings and etchings, and the undated works can be placed in sequence fairly easily. In the controversy among art historians over the authenticity of a great number of paintings ascribed to Rembrandt, even the most critical selection cannot gainsay the acknowledged course of development in his work. The rather extensive information that exists concerning Rembrandt's life is generally accepted as having a direct bearing on his development as artist. This has occasionally led to an extremely romantic interpretation of his work. Without denying the relationship between life and work, recent scholars have attempted a more sober approach – an objectification, if you will, of the romantic view, which was based partly on incorrect data and partly on an impulse to idealize as a human being the creator of such an imposing oeuvre.

It is interesting to contemplate the extent to which Rembrandt's activity and development as draftsman agree with the current image of him as painter. We shall therefore look briefly at the various phases into which his life and work have been divided.

In the society of the seventeenth century, Rembrandt's father belonged, as owner of a grain mill in Leiden, to the group we might now classify as prosperous middle-class. In any event, he was rich enough to give Rembrandt, who was born in 1606, an excellent education. After having attended the Latin School, where he at least received thorough instruction in Latin and the classical literature, Rembrandt enrolled in 1620 at Leiden University. Just what his intention in doing so was, and whether he ever actually began an academic study, remains uncertain.

Be that as it may, a short time later he became a pupil of the Leiden painter Jacob Isaäcsz. van Swanenburgh. Although the artistic influence of this first master cannot be traced even in Rembrandt's earliest known works, it can be assumed that Rembrandt spent a useful three or four years under his tutelage.

Swanenburgh, son of a Leiden burgomaster, was a cultivated man who had traveled and studied several years in Italy.

About 1624-25 Rembrandt completed his studies under Pieter Lastman in Amsterdam. The choice of this second master was exceedingly important. Lastman was a history painter, that is, a painter of biblical, mythological, and allegorical pictures, and was highly respected by his contemporaries. To become a good history painter, it was necessary to have a thorough knowledge of the Bible and of the stories from the classics and ancient history. Such a study also set the highest standards for the imagination and technical proficiency. Pupils must be qualified alike in painting the human figure and landscape, architecture and objects, while the ability to create a good composition and to express the quintessence of a story was requisite for success.

Rembrandt wanted to be a history painter, and here his schooling stood him in good stead. In 1625, after his study under Lastman, he returned to his birthplace Leiden and established himself as an independent painter. With this, the first phase of his career reached its end. Unfortunately, no works from this period are now known.

From 1625 until approximately the end of 1631, Rembrandt remained in Leiden, presumably sharing a studio with the somewhat younger Jan Lievens (1607-1674), who had also studied under Lastman. Lievens was a precocious young man, and it may be assumed that the two youthful artists stimulated one another. This Leiden period, certainly as far as the first years are concerned, must be regarded as an advanced term of study. Rembrandt's earliest dated paintings are often rather clumsily executed. Lastman's influence is easy to discern.

In Rembrandt's drawings, the element of experimentation and the desire to master technique in order to be a good history painter are strongly evident. The human figure and the rendering of emotions in face and gesture absorb him, and very soon he introduces a play of light and dark to enhance the effects he is seeking. The earliest little self-portrait (plate 1) is thus a study of the fall of light on a face – his own face, but that was of secondary importance. There are other early sketches made from life, of passersby in the street (plates 2, 3), and studies for paintings (plate 4) and etchings (plate 5). A drawing of a *Raising of Lazarus,* which he changed into an *Entombment* as he was working on it (plate 6), is a good example of a compositional study altered during execution. After five years in Leiden, Rembrandt had become an accomplished artist, as attested by any number of paintings, etchings, and drawings – see, for example, his *Jeremiah* reproduced on page 24.

Rembrandt moved to Amsterdam in 1631 most likely for two reasons: the city

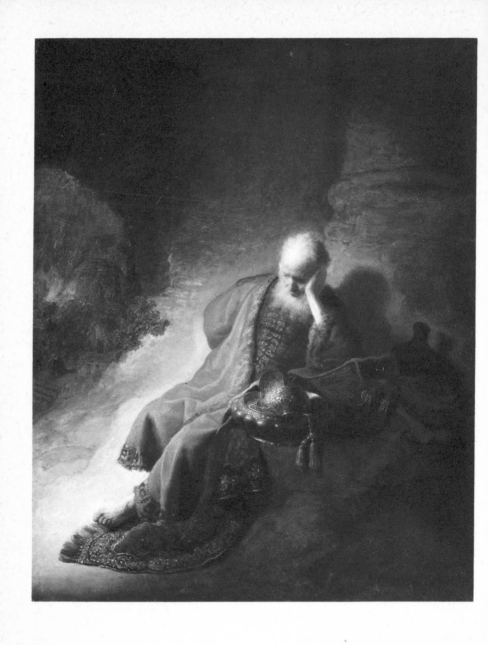

Jeremiah Lamenting the Destruction of Jerusalem, 1630. Panel, 58 x 46 cm. Rijksmuseum, Amsterdam

offered far more varied artistic opportunities, and the economic possibilities were much greater there than in Leiden. His first important work in Amsterdam was *The Anatomy Lesson of Dr. Tulp* (see page 26). He was commissioned to portray the praelector in anatomy of the Surgeons' Guild, Dr. Tulp, with several other members of the guild. The result is most remarkable. Rembrandt seems not only to have developed himself as history painter but also as portrait-ist – and without the benefit of commissions, for the only portraits known from his Leiden period are of himself and his family. Moreover, he solves in an original way the difficult task of composing a group portrait, and he knows how to attain an unprecedented element of liveliness. With this one canvas he joins the ranks of the best portrait painters in the city. Lucrative portrait commissions stream his way.

Meanwhile, his aspirations as history painter continue unabated. He receives an important commission from the Stadholder, Prince Frederick Henry of Orange, to paint a series of Passion scenes. In addition, he makes a number of large pictures which clearly manifest his striving for a Baroque exuberance, for a dramatic rendering of human emotions conveyed by every gesture and move-ment (see page 27).

During this period his drawings show a great diversity of subject matter and technique. The striving for liveliness is expressed in the treatment of the theme (plate 8) and in the wielding of the line as well (plates 15, 22). In other drawings we see Rembrandt going to work in a very different way. The chosen subject seems to determine his manner of drawing. For the little portrait of Saskia (colorplate 1), he elects to use the most delicate technique of silverpoint on vellum, drawing with the greatest care and subtlety. Another time, when he makes a rapid sketch of Saskia looking out of a window (plate 11), he ignores every detail and achieves just what he wants with a few lines, invoking a strong sense of light by placing the small figure against the dark space inside the window.

Rembrandt works in so many different ways that we are amazed by his versatility. To some extent the subject matter he draws is directly related to the paintings, but he seems to have limited certain motifs to the drawings – the scenes of domestic life, for instance, something of which can be found only fragmentarily in the paintings. On the other hand, very little preliminary work for his activities as portrait painter can be discovered in the drawings.

His personal circumstances in these years were for the most part felicitous. In 1634 he married the wealthy Saskia van Uylenburgh, and in 1639 they purchased a large house on Sint-Anthoniebreestraat. Already, it seems, Rembrandt had begun building up a collection, undoubtedly a sign of prosperity and ambition

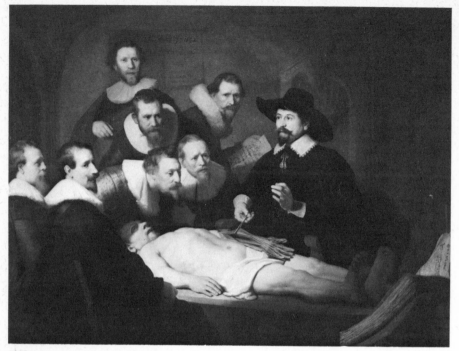

The Anatomy Lesson of Dr. Nicolaes Tulp, 1632. Canvas, 162.5 x 216.5 cm. Mauritshuis, The Hague

for social status. At that time a collection consisted not only of art but also of weapons, sea shells, plants, and "rarities."

It is a common tendency to try to divide the life of an artist into periods. The end of Rembrandt's first successful years in Amsterdam is therefore generally considered to coincide with the death of Saskia and the completion of *The Night Watch,* both of which occurred in 1642. In many ways this line of argument does not hold up, since *The Night Watch* was not rejected by those who had commissioned it, as is often maintained, and since it is dangerous to link Rembrandt's personal loss with a turnabout in his work. Nonetheless, this year is not ill-chosen. *The Night Watch,* or rather *The Company of Captain Frans Banning Cocq,* one of several civic-guard pieces ordered for the newly completed hall of the arquebusiers, can indeed be regarded as a conclusion to Rembrandt's most Baroque period. Thereafter a change can be observed in his paintings. He begins to use canvases of a smaller size, forsakes the attempt to render a maximum of movement, and produces less work.

Yet the dividing line of 1642 is more vulnerable when it comes to the etchings and drawings. A search for simplicity is evident in the etchings even before 1640, and the great variety of the drawings makes it virtually impossible to speak of any clear turning. For all intents and purposes, however, the years 1640-42 form a defensible boundary of the first Amsterdam period.

The phase that follows is more difficult to describe. More vigorous activity in drawing seems to compensate for Rembrandt's diminished productivity in painting. The painting themselves are less ambitious in design and simpler in subject matter: the *Young Girl at a Window* of 1645 is a good example (see page 29). In his history pieces, Rembrandt pays more attention to detail. Yet a clear characterization of his manner of painting cannot be given, for it varies greatly. In the drawings we see a remarkable number of biblical scenes (plates 38, 40, 41, 43, for example), but now more subdued in movement. Particularly after 1645, his

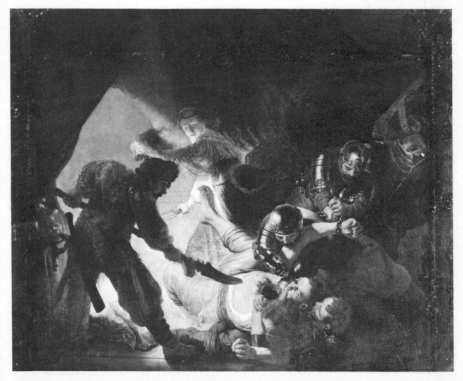

The Blinding of Samson, 1636. Canvas, 236 x 302 cm. Städelsches Kunstinstitut, Frankfurt am Main

27

interest in landscape increases strongly, a phenomenon which had manifested itself somewhat earlier in his etchings.

Rembrandt's domestic situation at this time was less than flourishing. The purchase of the large house had been over-optimistic, and he failed to keep up his mortgage payments. His affair with Geertge Dircx, a childless young widow hired to care for Titus after Saskia died, may at first have seemed pleasant enough, but it did not last. Partly because of the arrival of Hendrikje Stoffels in the household, the relationship between Rembrandt and Geertge steadily deteriorated, and in 1649 it led to an explosion. Rembrandt barely escaped a forced marriage with Geertge. His successful attempt to have her confined to a house of correction in Gouda casts a reprehensible light on his character. Rembrandt never married Hendrikje, but she remained true to him until her death in 1662. In 1654 their daughter Cornelia was born.

In searching for a transition between the second Amsterdam period and the third, in which Rembrandt's activities as painter once more increased and his manner of painting again became more homogeneous, one is struck by the year 1649 because it seems to mark a nadir in his creativity: not one single painting, not one single etching bears that year's date.

Whether or not the unhappy domestic situation had an influence on Rembrandt's ability to work, his steadily worsening financial position, which in 1656 would lead to his insolvency, most certainly did not. Even in the years when his whole art collection was auctioned off and he had to leave the house in the Breestraat for much more modest quarters on the Rozengracht, his work shows no sign of diminished productivity or quality. On the contrary, the years 1650 to 1662 are among the richest in his entire career. No fewer than three large commissions were granted him: *The Anatomy Lesson of Dr. Deyman* in 1656, *The Sampling Officials* in 1661, and *The Conspiracy of the Batavians* for the new Amsterdam Town Hall in 1661-62. Even though this last commission ultimately proved disastrous (the painting having been rejected, Rembrandt cut away all but the central section), the three commissions are nonetheless strong evidence that Rembrandt was still esteemed by his contemporaries.

We have already seen that after 1645 the landscape began to play an important part in his drawings. This lasted until about 1655. In the landscape drawings, which Rembrandt must have done directly from nature, it is clear that he sought to confine himself to the essence. By using the simplest means as he sketched on his wanderings, and by eliminating a great deal, he faultlessly succeeded in capturing the character of the Dutch polder landscape, of the Amstel and the IJ, of the farms usually hidden among trees (plates 53, 62, 74, 76). In the biblical scenes, too, we encounter the art of elimination (plate 52) and Rembrandt's

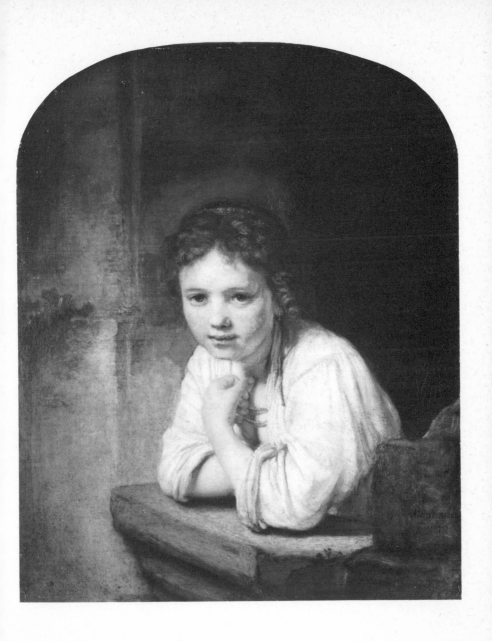

Young Girl at a Window, 1645. Canvas, 77.5 × 62.5 cm. Dulwich College Picture Gallery, London

steadily increasing ability to render the spiritual tension of the story.

In tracing Rembrandt's development, it does not seem justified to keep to a dividing line of about 1650 for the drawings. The changes take place gradually, and all the while he also reaches back now and then to techniques and means of expression which he had used in earlier years. On the whole it can be said that this drawing method aimed less and less at the rendering of flowing forms, at anything that might be called charming. Angular contours and scraggy figures begin to dominate, and the power which continually emanates from the drawing is concentrated on a monumental interaction of the forms (plates 89, 95). Yet, as we have said, Rembrandt returns without hesitation to earlier means of expression: to depict the body of a sleeping girl (plate 85), he seizes the flowing brush.

During the last period of his life, from 1662 up to his death in 1669, Rembrandt limited himself nearly exclusively to painting. Several of his greatest masterpieces date from these years – *The Jewish Bride,* for example, and the marvelous self-portraits of 1669, one of which is reproduced on page 31. Yet while he continued painting with the brush up to the very end, he totally abandoned the etching needle and used chalk or his drawing pen only to set down a few ideas (plates 94, 95).

The greatness of Rembrandt as draftsman lies in the combination of a number of qualities and certainly also in his determination to look anew at each subject and each situation in and of itself. He never repeated himself or lapsed into affectation. Unlike his paintings and his etchings, his drawings were hardly ever for display or sale. Therefore they give the most intimate view of his artistic mastery.

Notes

1 C. Hofstede de Groot, *Die Urkunden über Rembrandt (1575-1721),* The Hague, 1906, p. 169.
2 *Urkunden,* p. 56.
3 A. Bredius, "Rembrandtiana," *Oud-Holland* 31 (1913), pp. 71-75.
4 O. Benesch, *The Drawings of Rembrandt: A Critical and Chronological Catalogue,* 6 vols., London/New York, 1954-57.
5 E. Haverkamp-Begemann, "Rembrandt as Teacher," in the catalogue *Rembrandt After Three Hundred Years,* The Art Institute of Chicago, 1969.
6 J. Q. van Regteren Altena, "Retouches aan ons Rembrandt-beeld I: De zogenaamde voorstudie voor de Anatomische les van Dr. Deyman," *Oud-Holland* LXV (1950), pp. 171-78.
7 B. Haak, "De nachtelijke samenzwering van Claudius Civilis in het Schakerbos op de Rembrandttentoonstelling te Amsterdam," *Antiek* IV (1969), pp. 136-48.
8 J. Bruyn, *Rembrandt's keuze van bijbelse onderwerpen,* Utrecht, 1959, and Ch. Tümpel, "Studien zur Ikonographie der Historien Rembrandts," *Nederlands Kunsthistorisch Jaarboek* 20 (1969), pp. 107-98.
9 F. Lugt, *Wandelingen met Rembrandt in en om Amsterdam,* Amsterdam, 1915.

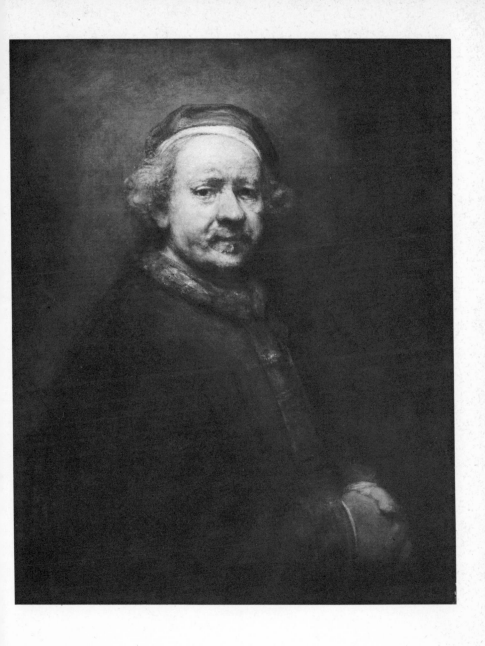

Self-Portrait, 1669. Canvas, 83 x 69 cm. National Gallery, London

The abbreviations in parentheses (B., Ba., Br.) at the end of each entry refer to the oeuvre catalogues of the drawings, etchings and paintings (see page 222).

1

Portrait of Saskia in a Straw Hat, 1633

Silverpoint on white prepared vellum, 185 x 107 mm
Inscribed by Rembrandt: This is drawn after my wife, when she was 21 years old, the third day after our betrothal, the 8th of June 1633
Kupferstichkabinett, Staatliche Museen, Berlin-Dahlem (B. 427). See pp. 20, 21, 25

2

Christ Among His Disciples, 1634

Black and red chalk, pen and brush, brown ink, washed in different tones, heightened with white, 335 x 476 mm
Signed and dated: Rembrandt. f. 1634
Teylers Museum, Haarlem (B. 89). See p. 16
The disciple in the middle is drawn on a separate piece of paper, which Rembrandt pasted on the sheet

dit is naer mijn huijsvrou geconterfeijt
do sij 21 jaer oudt was den derden
dach als wij getroudt waeren

Rembrandt
1633

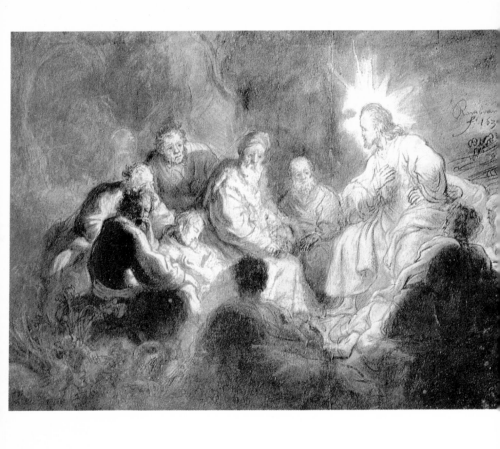

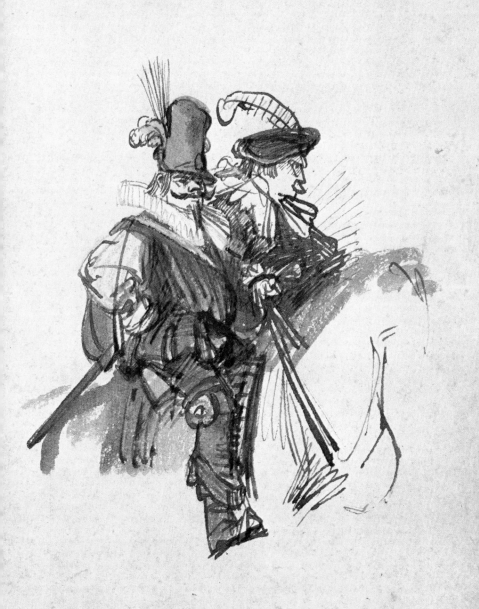

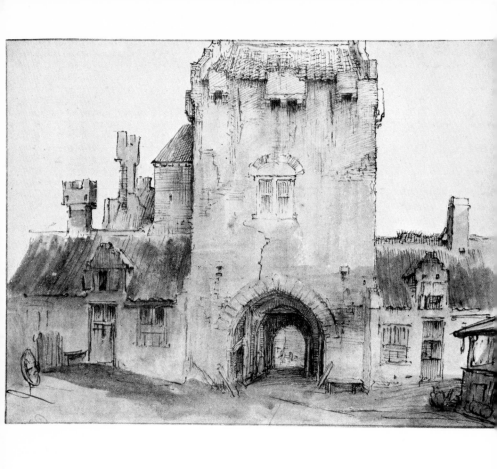

3

Two Mummers on Horseback, c. 1637-38

Pen and brush, brown ink, yellow and red chalk, some white, 212 x 153 mm
The Pierpont Morgan Library, New York (B. 368)

4

The West Gate of Rhenen, c. 1647-48

Pen and brush, brown ink, touches of white, 165 x 226 mm
Teylers Museum, Haarlem (B. 826). See p. 21

I

Self-Portrait, c. 1627–28

Pen and brush, brown and gray ink, 127×95 mm
British Museum, London (B. 53). See pp. 20, 23

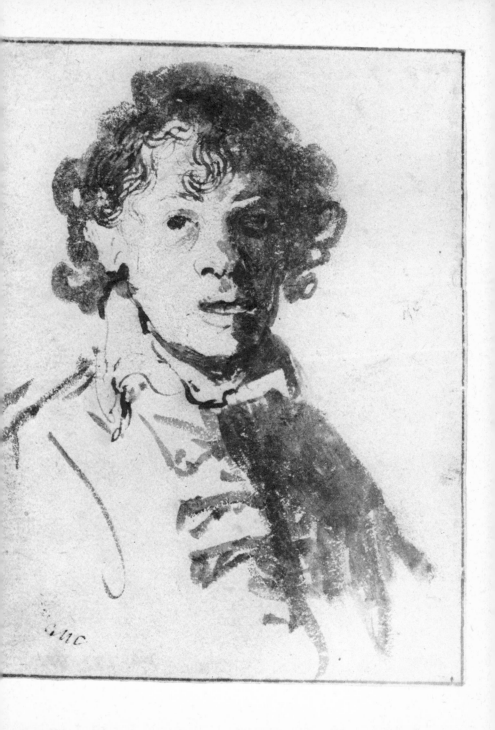

2

Standing Beggar, c. 1629

Black chalk, 290 x 167 mm
Rijksprentenkabinet, Amsterdam (B. 31)

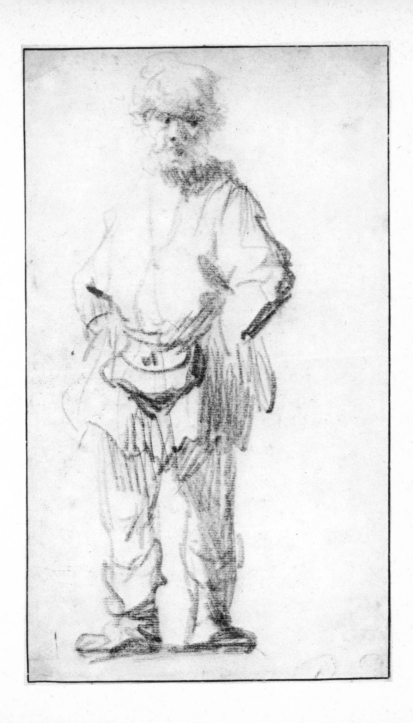

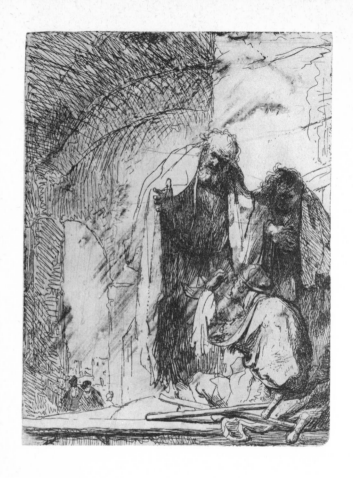

3a

Sts. Peter and John at the Gate of the Temple, c. 1629

Etching, 221 x 169 mm (Ba. 95)

3

Old Man with His Arms Extended, c. 1629

Black chalk, 254 x 190 mm
Kupferstichkabinett, Dresden (B. 12). See p. 18

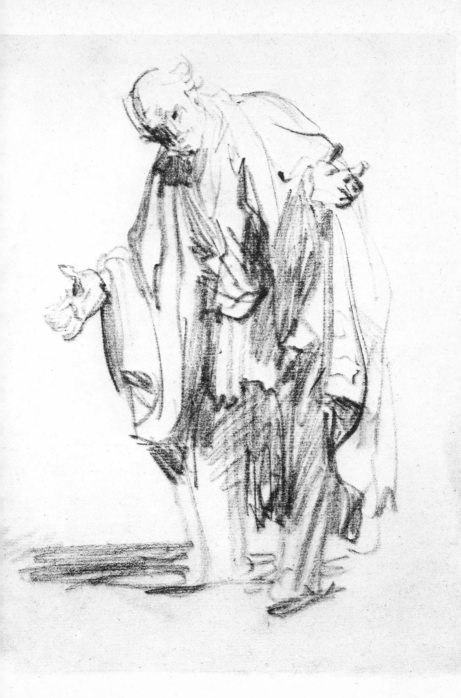

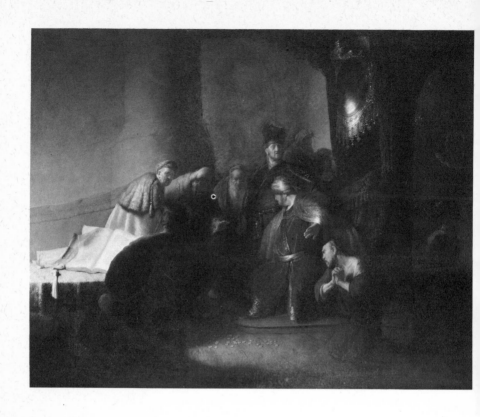

4a

Judas Returning the Thirty Pieces of Silver, 1629

Panel, 79.5 x 102 cm
Signed and dated
Private collection (Br. 539A)

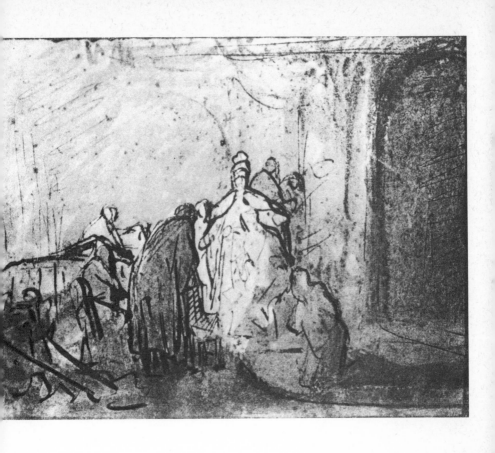

4

Judas Returning the Thirty Pieces of Silver, c. 1629

Study for plate 4a
Pen and brush, brown and gray ink, 112 x 145 mm
Private collection (B. 8). See pp. 13, 17

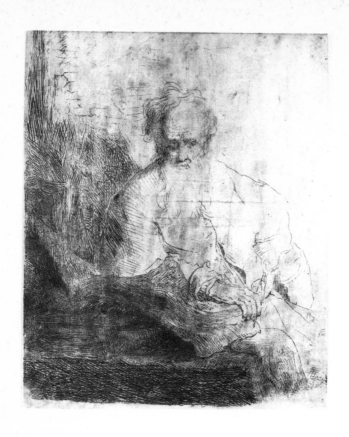

5a

St. Paul, c. 1629

Etching, 238 x 200 mm (Ba. 149)

5

St. Paul, c. 1629

Study for plate 5a
Red chalk and wash in gray ink, heightened with white, 236 x 201 mm
Louvre, Paris (B. 15). See p. 23

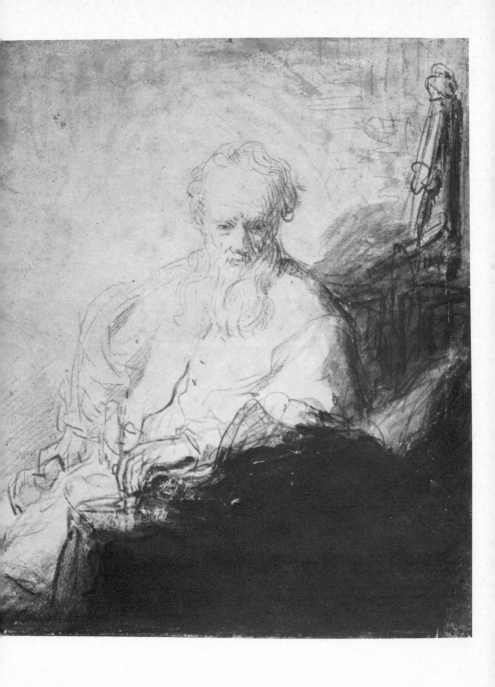

6

The Entombment, 1630

Red chalk, heightened with white, 280 x 203 mm
British Museum, London (B. 17). See p. 23

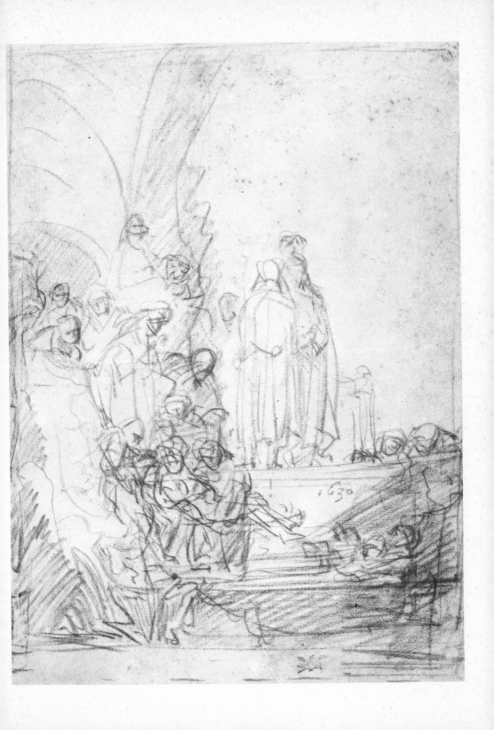

7

Young Woman at Her Toilet, c. 1632-34

Pen and brush, brown and gray ink, 238 x 184 mm
Albertina, Vienna (B. 395)

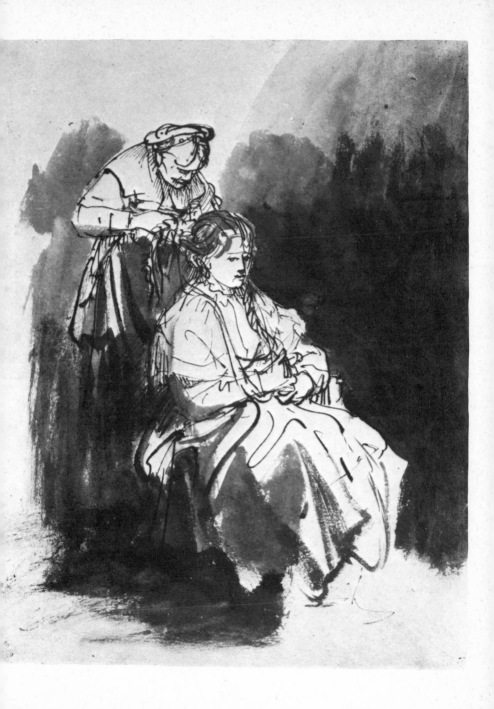

8

Christ Walking on the Waves. c. 1632-33

Pen, brown ink, 168 x 265 mm
British Museum, London (B. 70). See p. 25

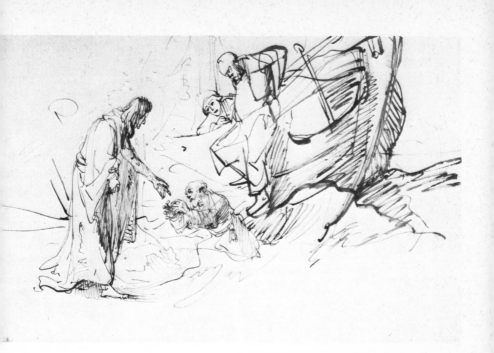

9

A Dromedary, c. 1633

Pen, brown ink, some white, 194 x 289 mm
Formerly Kunsthalle, Bremen (disappeared during World War II) (B. 453). See p. 20
Inscribed by another hand: Drommedaris. Rembrandt fecit. 633. Amsterdam.

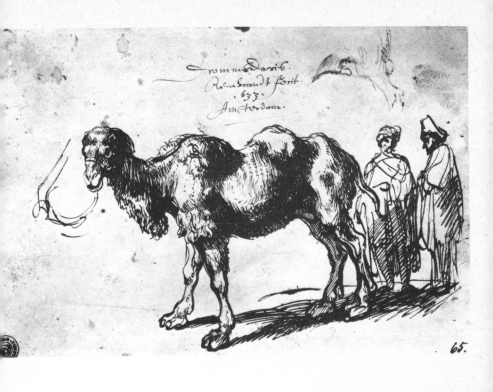

Dromedaris.
Rembrandt fecit.
1633.
Amsterdam.

65.

10

Studies of a Beggar and of an Old Woman with a Child, c. 1633-34

Pen and brush, brown ink, some white, 218 x 186 mm
Kupferstichkabinett, Staatliche Museen, Berlin-Dahlem (B. 218). See p. 18

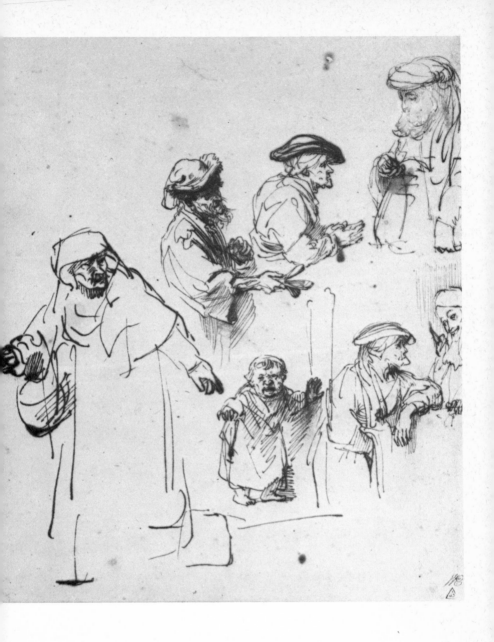

11

Saskia Looking Out of a Window, c. 1633-34

Pen and brush, brown ink, 236 x 178 mm
Museum Boymans-van Beuningen, Rotterdam (B. 250). See pp. 20, 25

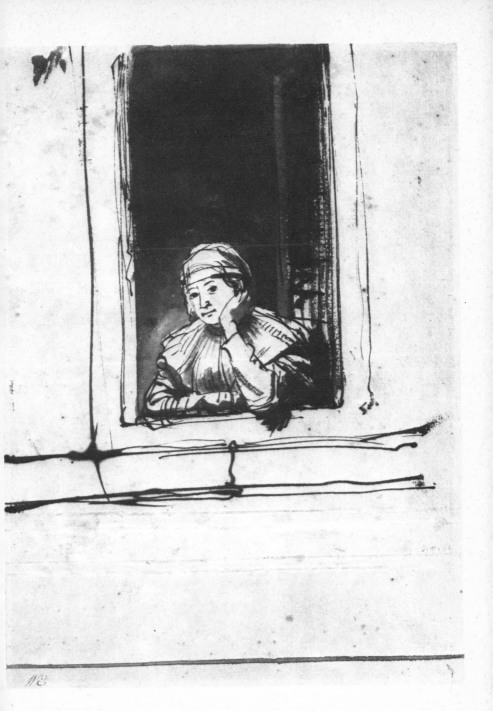

Portrait of a Man in an Armchair, 1634

Black and red chalk, pen and brush, brown ink, on vellum, 373 x 272 mm
Signed and dated: Rembrandt. f. 1634
Collection Mrs. Charles Payson, New York (B. 433). See pp. 16, 21

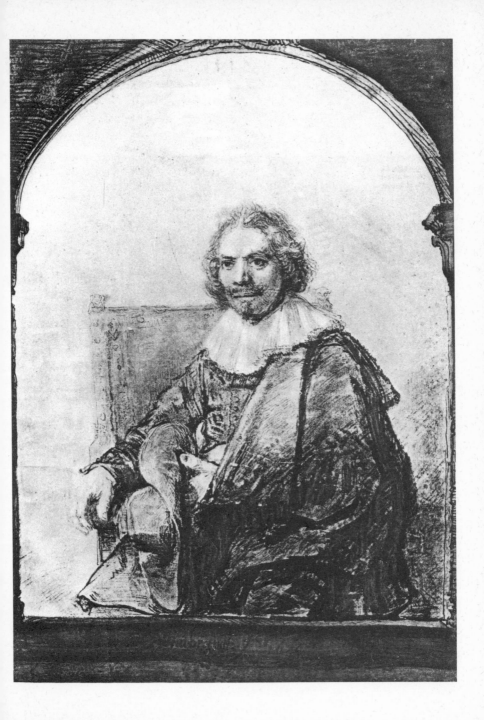

13

Study for an Adoration of the Magi, c. 1634-35

Pen, brown ink, 177 x 159 mm
Rijksprentenkabinet, Amsterdam (B. 115)

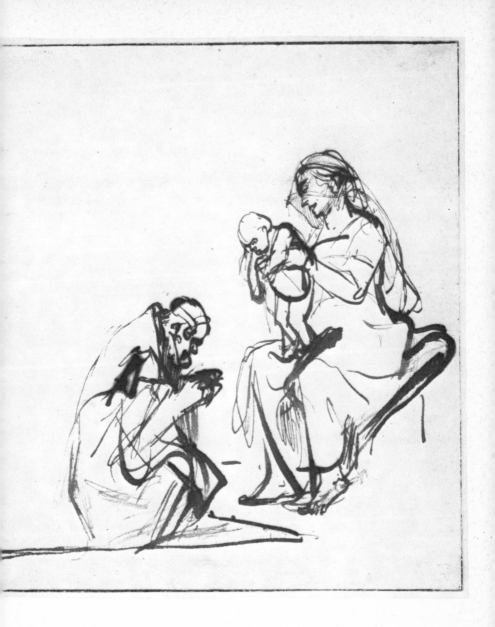

14

The Naughty Child, c. 1635

Pen and brush, brown ink, some white, 206 x 143 mm
Kupferstichkabinett, Staatliche Museen, Berlin-Dahlem (B. 401)
See pp. 18, 19
Signed by a later hand: Rembrant

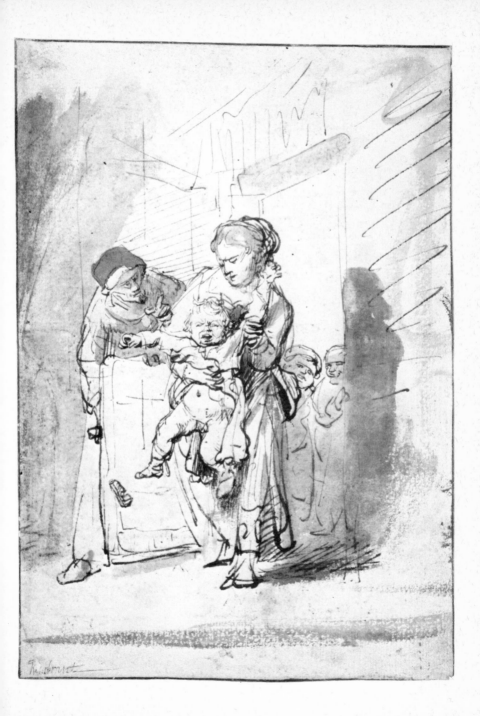

15

Actor in Dialogue with a Kneeling Man, c. 1635

Pen and brush, brown ink, 182 x 153 mm
Rijksprentenkabinet, Amsterdam (B. 293). See p. 25

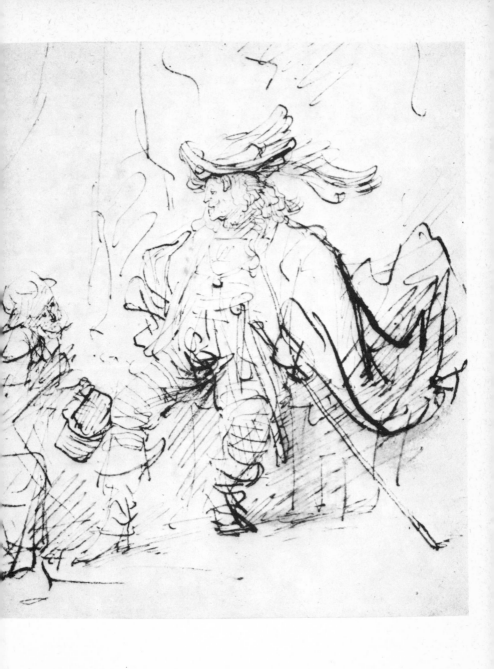

16

The Last Supper (after Leonardo da Vinci), c. 1635

Red chalk, 365 x 475 mm
Signed: Rembrant. f.
The Lehmann Collection, New York (B. 443). See p. 18

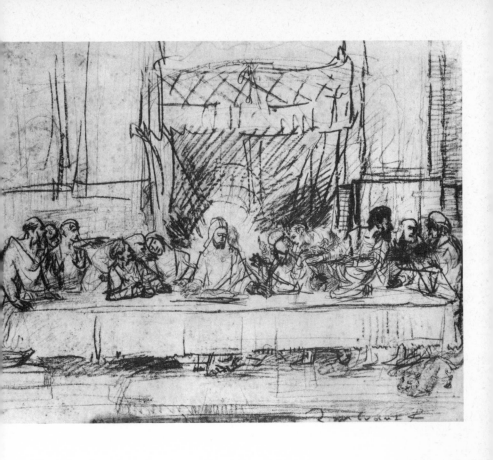

17

Woman with a Child Frightened by a Dog, c. 1636

Pen, brown ink, 184 x 146 mm
Museum of Fine Arts, Budapest (B. 411). See pp. 18, 19
Signed by a later hand: Rembrant

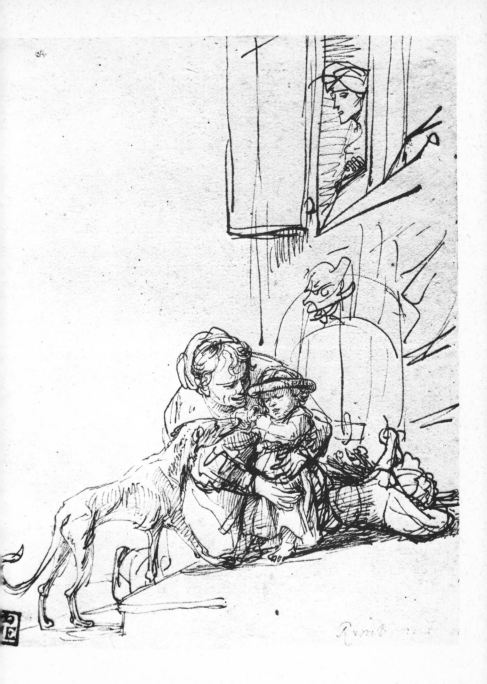

18

Woman Carrying a Child Downstairs, c. 1636

Pen and brush, brown ink, 187 x 133 mm
The Pierpont Morgan Library, New York (B. 313). See pp. 18, 20

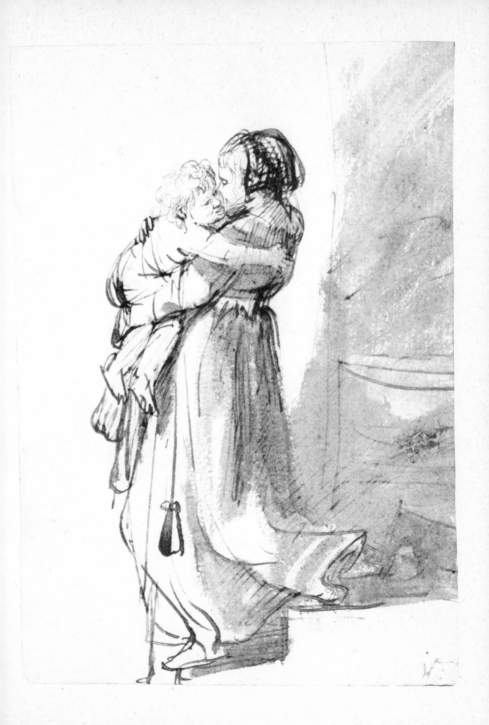

19

Studies of an Old Man in a Long Coat, c. 1636

Pen, brown ink, 152 x 185 mm
British Museum, London (B. 327). See p. 18

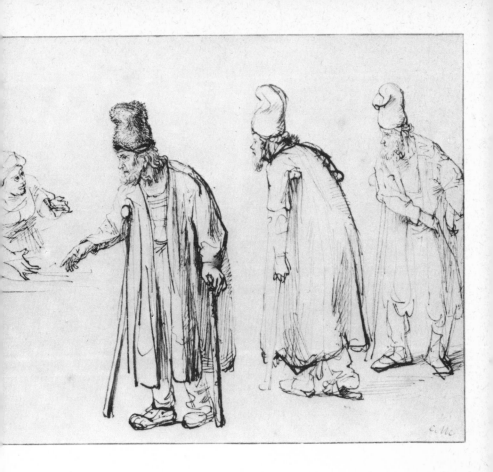

20

Farmhouse in Sunlight, c. 1636

Pen and brush, brown ink, 165 x 223 mm
Museum of Fine Arts, Budapest (B. 463)
Signed by a later hand: Rembrant

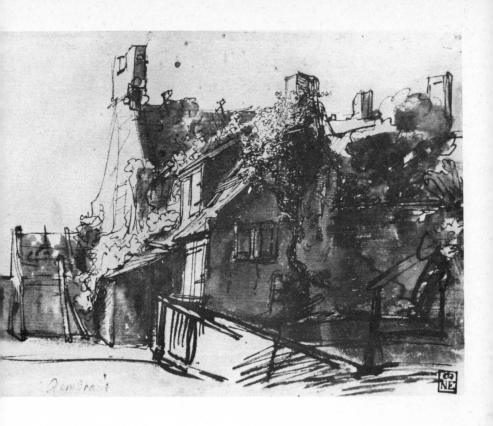

21

An Elephant, 1637

Black chalk, 230 x 340 mm
Signed and dated: Rembrandt ft. 1637
Albertina, Vienna (B. 457). See p. 20

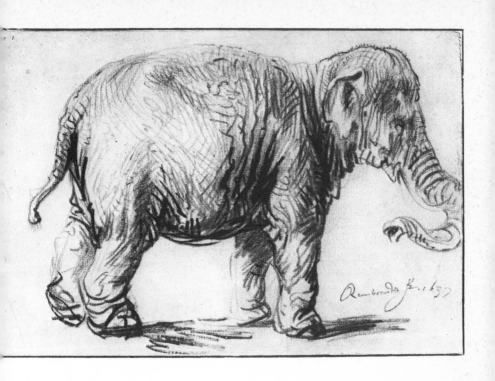

22

Susanna and the Elders, c. 1637-38

Pen, brown ink, 149 x 177 mm
Kupferstichkabinett, Staatliche Museen, Berlin-Dahlem (B. 159)

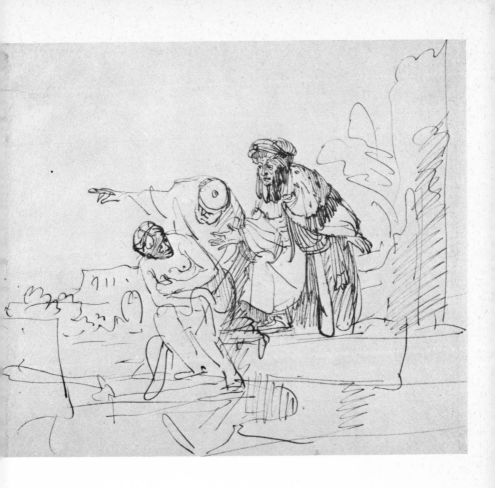

23
Christ as a Gardener Appears to Mary Magdalen, c. 1638 (?)

Study for plate 24a
Pen, brown ink, 153 x 146 mm
Rijksprentenkabinet, Amsterdam (B. 538)

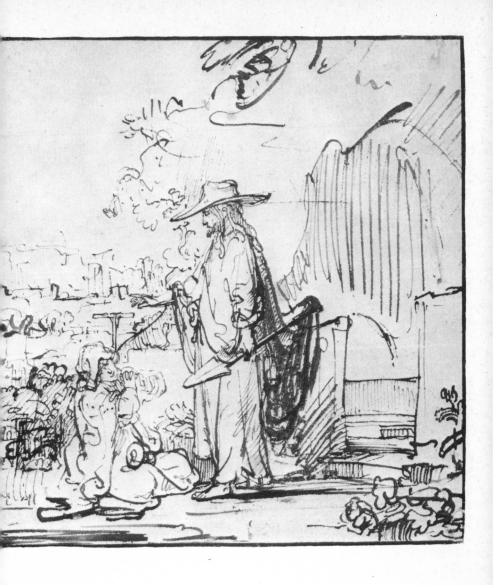

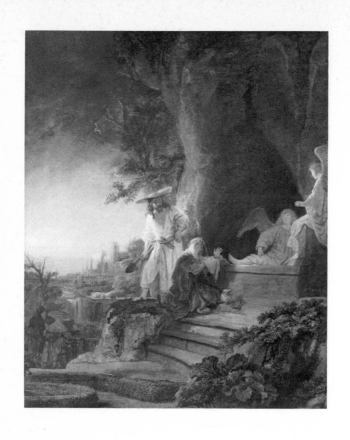

24a

Christ as a Gardener Appears to Mary Magdalen, 1638

Panel, 51.5 x 50 cm
Signed and dated
Buckingham Palace, London (Br. 559)

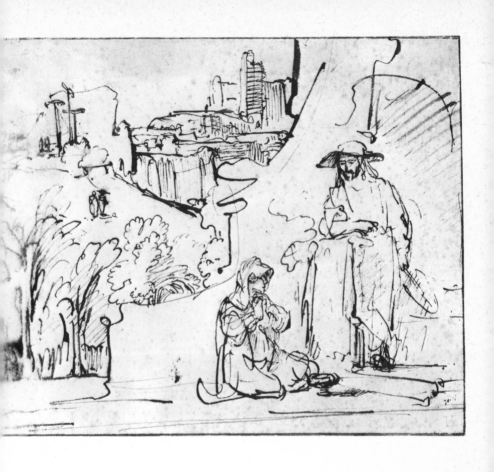

24

Christ as a Gardener Appears to Mary Magdalen, c. 1638 (?)

Study for plate 24a
Pen, brown ink, 152 x 190 mm
Rijksprentenkabinet, Amsterdam (B. 537)

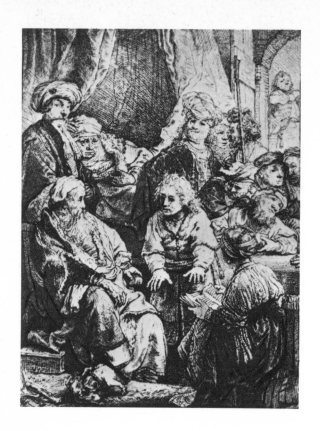

25a

Joseph Telling His Dreams, 1638

Etching, 110 x 83 mm
Signed and dated (Ba. 37)

25

Studies of a Woman Reading and an Oriental, c. 1638

Pen and brush, brown ink, some white, 139 x 125 mm
Collection Werner H. Kramarsky, New York (B. 168). See p. 18
Both figures are used in the etching, plate 25a

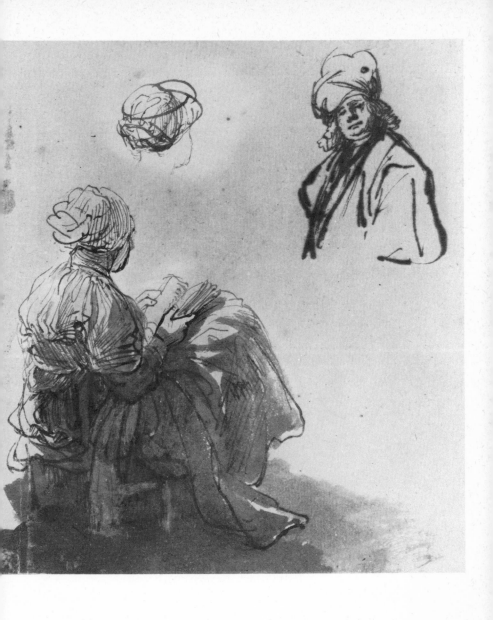

26

Woman in North Holland Costume, c. 1638-40

Pen and brush, brown ink, 220 x 154 mm
Teylers Museum, Haarlem (B. 315)
On the reverse, in an 18th-century handwriting: De Minne moer van Titus soon van Rembra[ndt]
(The nurse of Titus, son of Rembrandt)

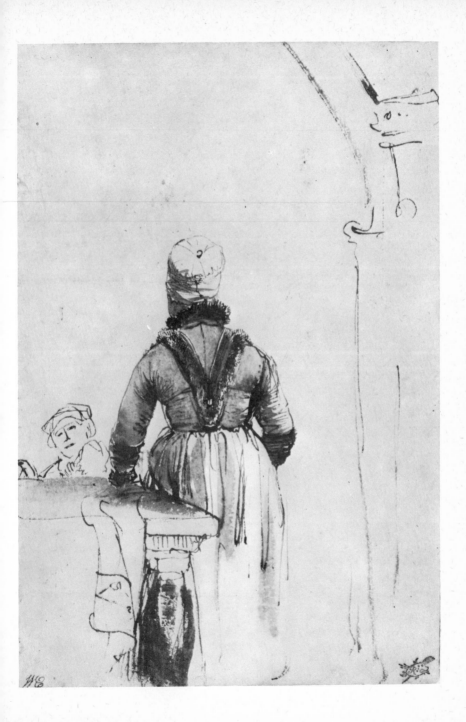

27

Manoah's Sacrifice, c. 1639

Pen, brown ink, 175 x 190 mm
Kupferstichkabinett, Staatliche Museen, Berlin-Dahlem (B. 180)

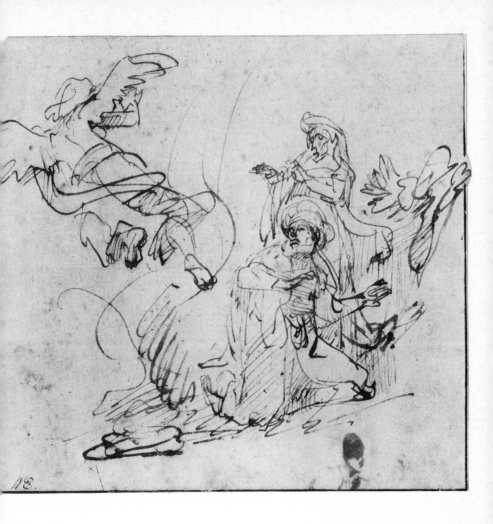

28

Portrait of Titia van Uylenburgh, 1639

Pen and brush, brown ink, 177 x 147 mm
Inscribed and dated by Rembrandt: Tijtsija van Ulenburch 1639
Nationalmuseum, Stockholm (B. 441)
Signed by a later hand: Rhimbrand
Titia van Uylenburgh was an elder sister of Saskia

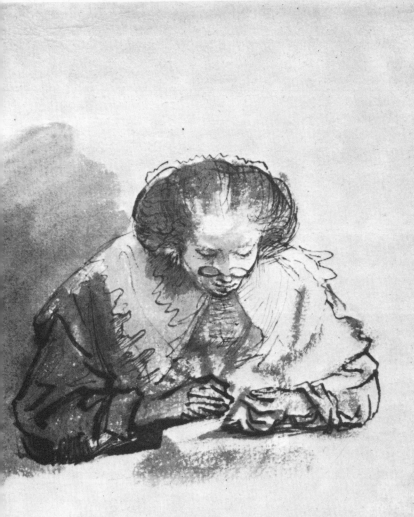

Sÿtsja van vlenbürg

1639

1877.

Rhembrandt ff

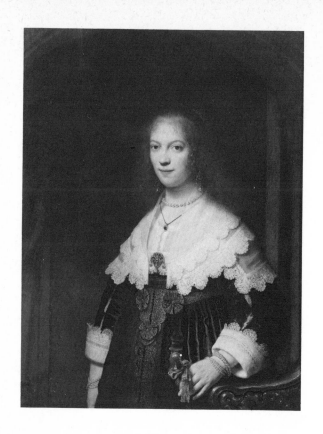

29a

Portrait of Maria Trip, 1639

Panel, 107 x 82 cm
Signed and dated
Rijksmuseum, Amsterdam (Br. 356)
Maria Trip (1619-1683) was the daughter of a rich Amsterdam merchant

29

Portrait of Maria Trip, c. 1639

Study for plate 29a
Pen and brush, brown ink, touches of red chalk, heightened with white, 160 x 128 mm
British Museum, London (B. 442). See p. 16

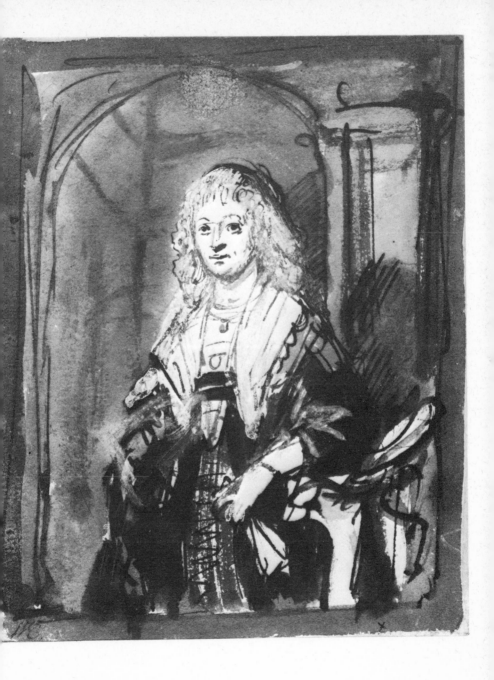

30

Saskia Sitting Up in Bed, c. 1639-40

Pen and brush, brown ink, 150 x 138 mm
Kupferstichkabinett, Dresden (B. 225). See p. 20

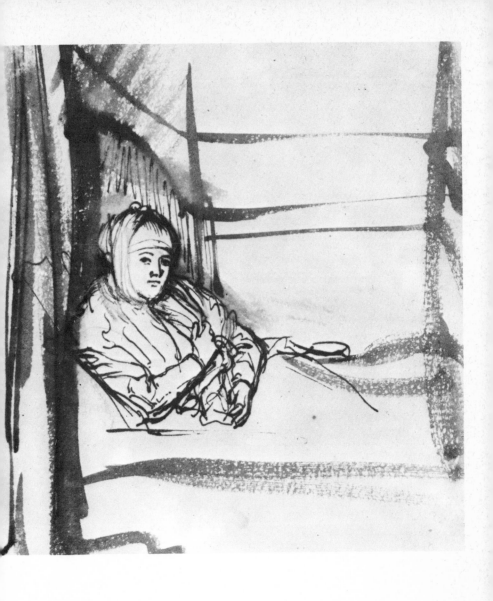

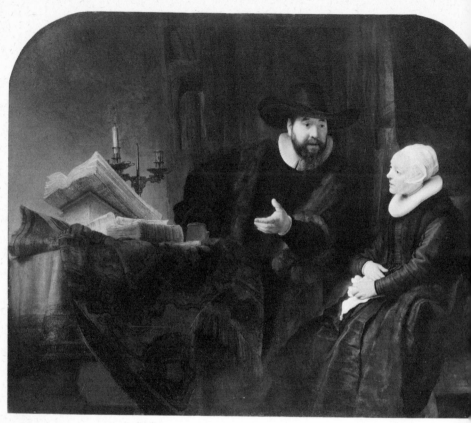

3 1a

Portrait of Cornelis Claesz. Anslo and a Woman, 1641

Canvas, 172 x 209 cm
Signed and dated
Gemäldegalerie, Staatliche Museen, Berlin-Dahlem (Br. 409)
Anslo (1592–1646) was a Mennonite preacher in Amsterdam

3 1

Portrait of Cornelis Claesz. Anslo, 1640

Study for plate 31a
Red chalk, pen and brush, brown and gray ink, heightened and corrected with white, 246 x 201 mm
Signed and dated: Rembrandt f. 1640
Louvre, Paris (B. 759). See p. 13

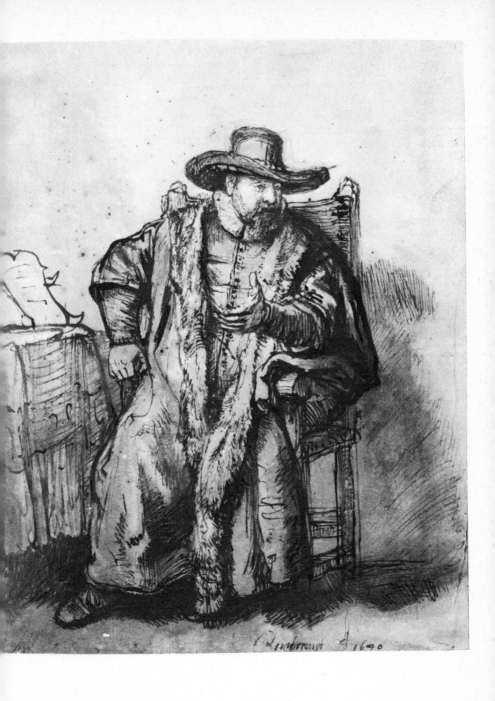

32

Bust of the Emperor Galba, after an antique sculpture, c. 1640-41

Pen, brown ink, 142 x 90 mm
Kupferstichkabinett, Staatliche Museen, Berlin-Dahlem (B. 770)

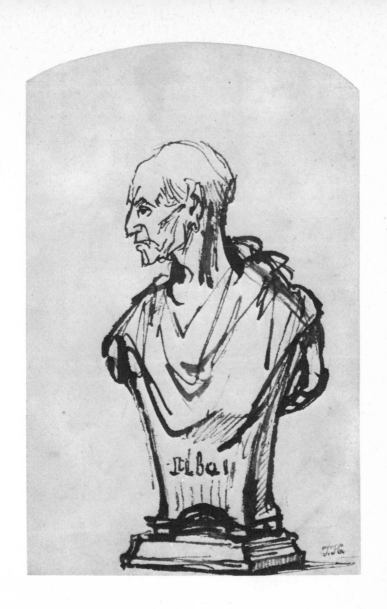

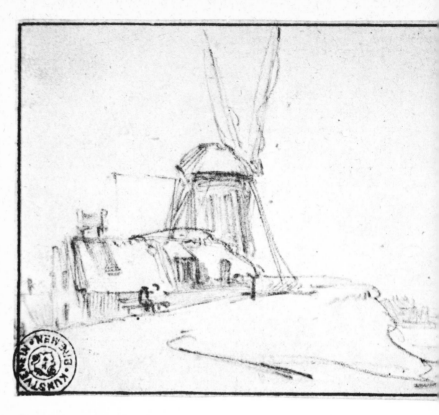

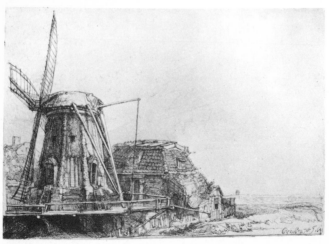

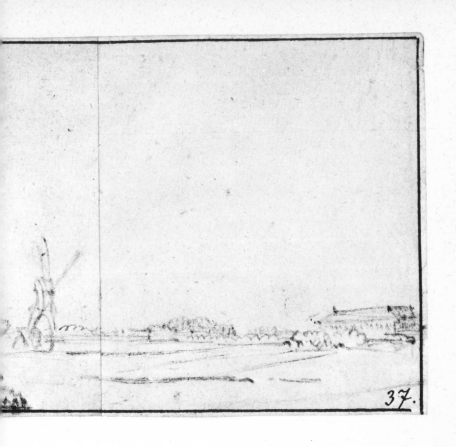

33

he Bulwark "De Passeerder" of Amsterdam; the Pest-Huis in the distance, c. 1640-41

Black chalk, on two sheets of paper, 85 x 231 mm
Kunsthalle, Bremen (B. 810)
The windmill is the same as on the etching, plate 33a

33a
The Windmill, 1641

Etching, 145 x 208 mm
Signed and dated (Ba. 233)

34

Satan Tempting Christ to Change Stones into Bread, c. 1640-42

Pen, brown ink, 185 x 220 mm
Staatliche Graphische Sammlung, Munich (B. 514)

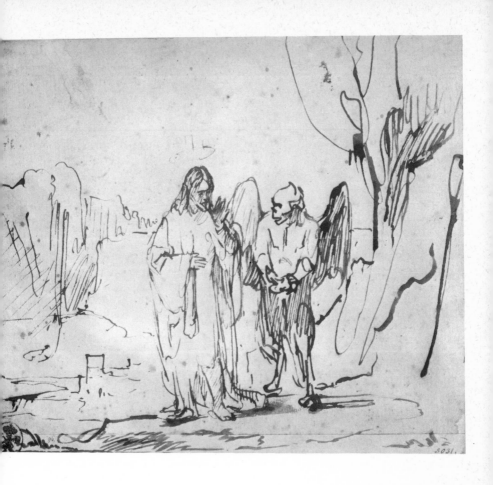

35
The Star of the Kings, c. 1641-42

Pen and brush, brown ink, one of the figures heightened with white, 204 x 323 mm
Signed: Rembrandt f.
British Museum, London (B. 736)

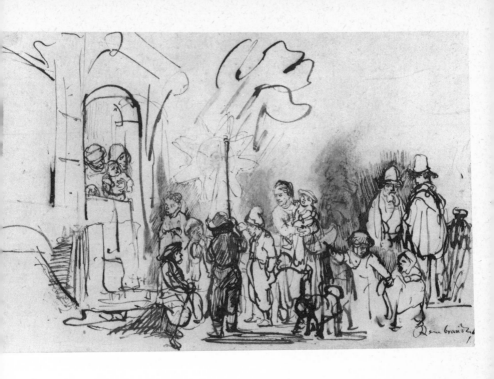

36
Study of a Pig, c. 1642-43

Pen, brown ink, 102 x 142 mm
British Museum, London (B. 778)

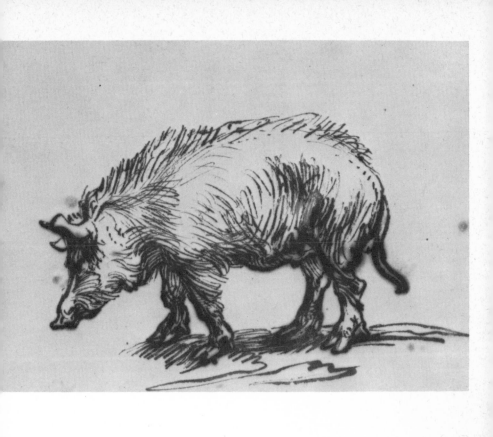

37
Jacob and Rachel Listening to an Account of Joseph's Dreams (?), c. 1642-43

Pen and brush, brown ink, heightened with white, 180 x 163 mm
British Museum, London (B. 528). See p. 19

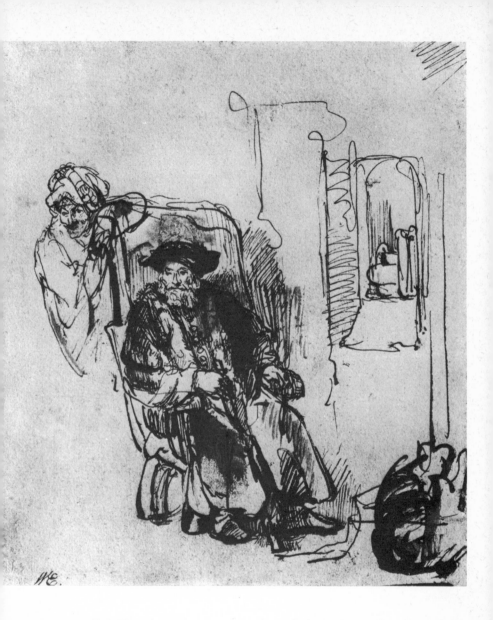

38
Joseph Telling His Dreams to Jacob, c. 1642–43

Pen and brush, brown ink, corrected with white, 175 x 245 mm
Signed: Rembrant f.
Albertina, Vienna (B. 526)

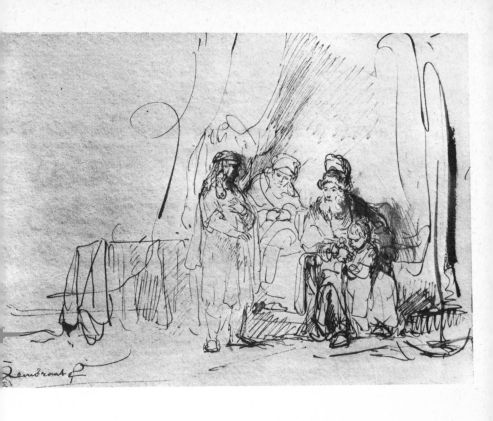

39

Mars and Venus Caught in a Net by Vulcan and Brought Before the Gods of Olympus, c. 1640-43

Pen, brown ink, 210 x 288 mm
Fodor Collection, Amsterdam (B. 540)

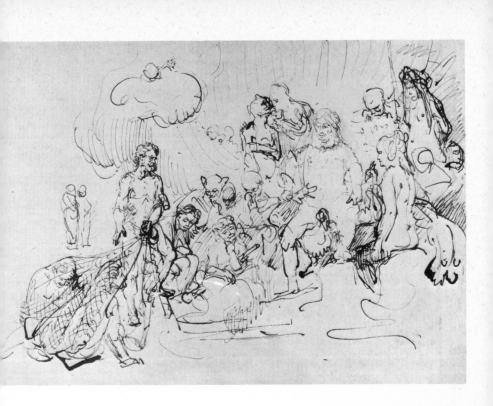

40

The Good Samaritan Arriving at the Inn, c. 1641-43

Pen and brush, brown ink, corrected with white, 184 x 287 mm
British Museum, London (B. 518a)

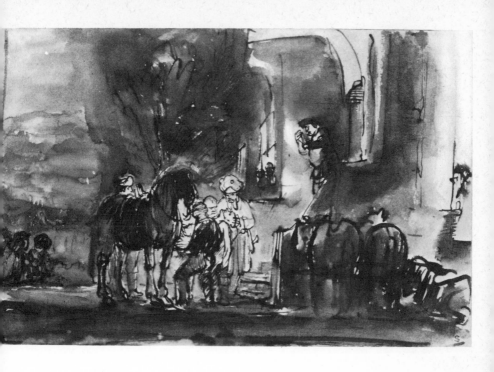

41

The Dismissal of Hagar and Ishmael, c. 1642-43

Pen and brush, brown ink, some white, 185 x 236 mm
British Museum, London (B. 524)
The figure of Abraham is drawn on a separate piece of paper, which Rembrandt pasted on the sheet

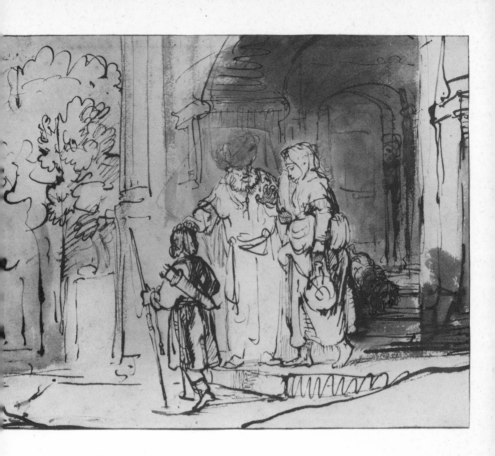

42

Tobias Frightened by the Fish, with the Angel, c. 1644

Pen and brush, brown ink, heightened with white, 205 x 273 mm
Kupferstichkabinett, Staatliche Museen, Berlin-Dahlem (B. 559)

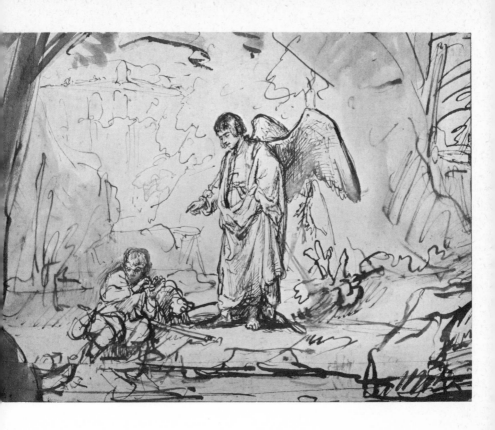

43
Esau Selling His Birthright to Jacob, c. 1644-45

Pen, brown ink, 155 x 148 mm
Fodor Collection, Amsterdam (B. 564)

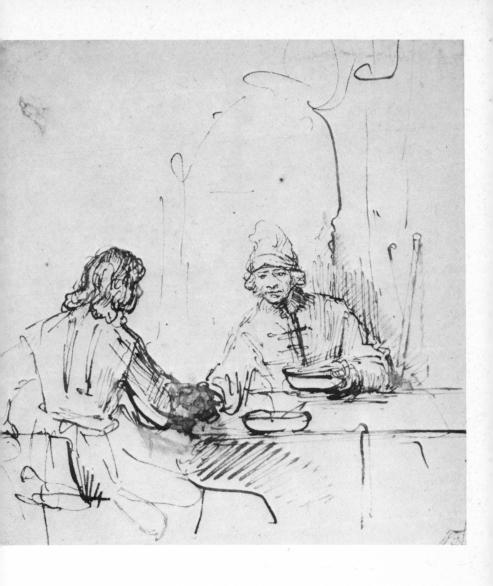

44

Young Man Pulling a Rope, c. 1645

Pen and brush, brown ink, heightened with white, 290 x 178 mm
Rijksprentenkabinet, Amsterdam (B. 311)

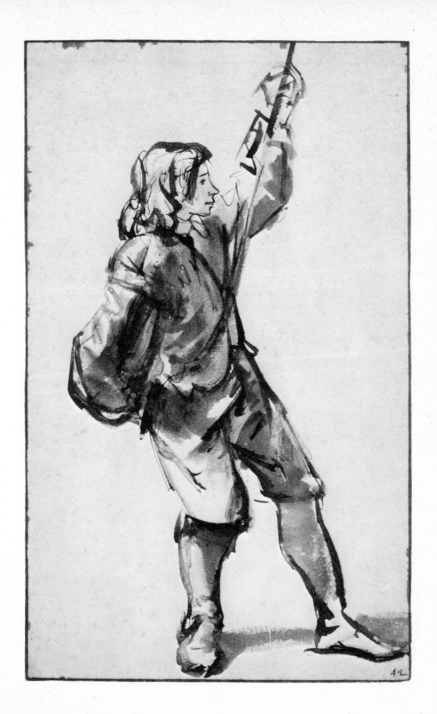

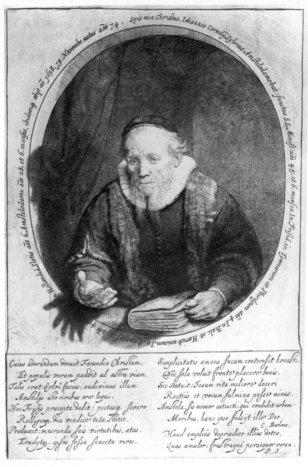

45a

Posthumous Portrait of Jan Cornelisz. Sylvius, 1646

Etching and burin, 278 x 188 mm
Signed and dated (Ba. 280)
Sylvius was a minister of the Dutch Reformed Church and preached in Amsterdam from 1610 until his death
in 1638. He was married to a cousin of Saskia.

45

Posthumous Portrait of Jan Cornelisz. Sylvius, c. 1646

Study for plate 45a
Pen and brush, brown ink, heightened with white, 284 x 194 mm
British Museum, London (B. 763). See p. 13

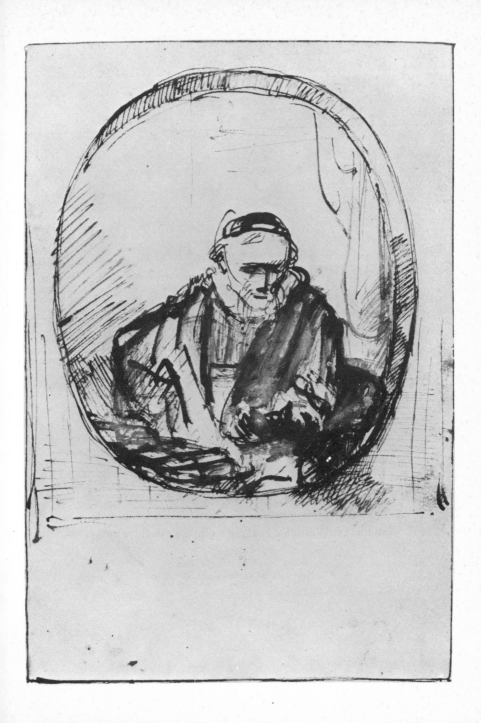

46

Study of a Woman Teaching a Child to Walk, c. 1646

Pen, brown ink, 160 x 165 mm
Nationalmuseum, Stockholm (B. 706)

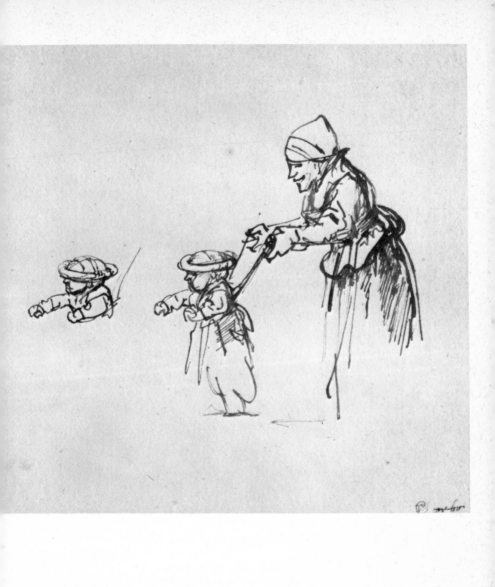

47

Elijah and the Prophets of Baal, c. 1647

Pen and brush, brown ink, 204 x 315 mm
Städtische Wessenberg-Gemäldegalerie, Constance (B. 593)

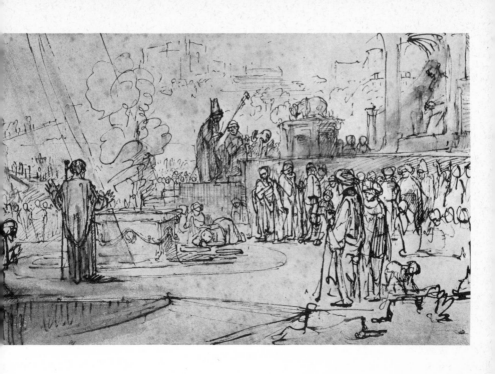

48

View of Rhenen, c. 1647-48

Pen and brush, brown ink, 210 x 324 mm
Bredius Museum, The Hague (B. 825). See p. 21

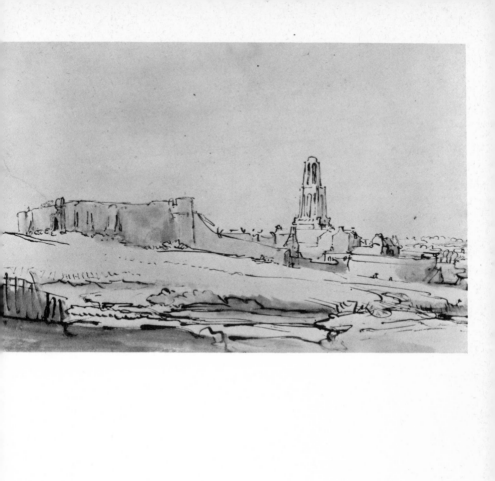

49

Beggar Couple with Children and a Dog, c. 1648

Black chalk, 105 x 100 mm
Albertina, Vienna (B. 751)

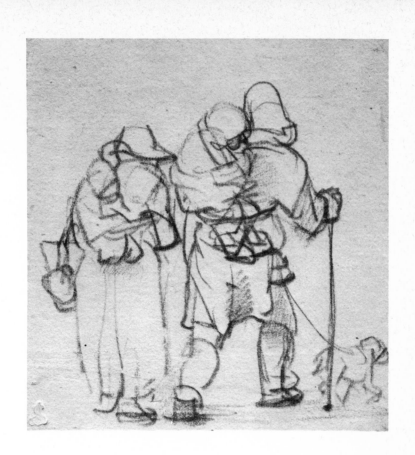

50

Christ Awaking the Apostles on the Mount of Olives, c. 1648-49

Pen and brush, brown ink, 166 x 261 mm
University Library, Warsaw (B. 613)

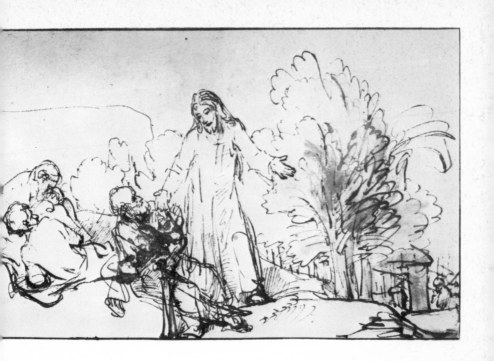

·

51
Christ and the Woman of Samaria, c. 1648-49

Pen, brown ink, 207 x 187 mm
Barber Institute of Fine Arts, Birmingham, England (B. 611)

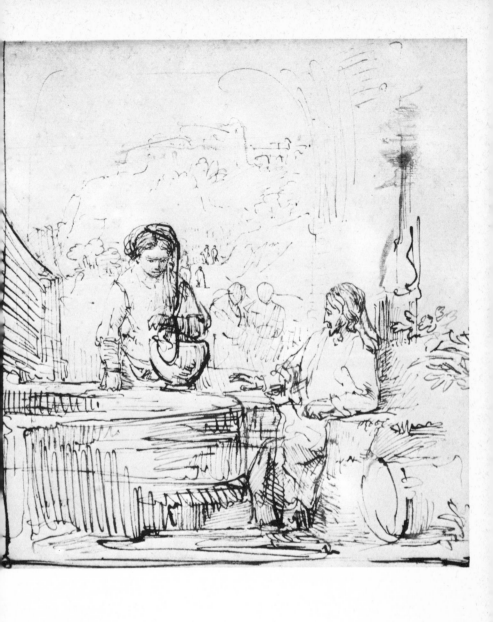

52

The Holy Family in the Carpenter's Workshop, c. 1648-49

Pen, brown ink, 173 x 227 mm
Museum Boymans-van Beuningen, Rotterdam (B. 620). See p. 28

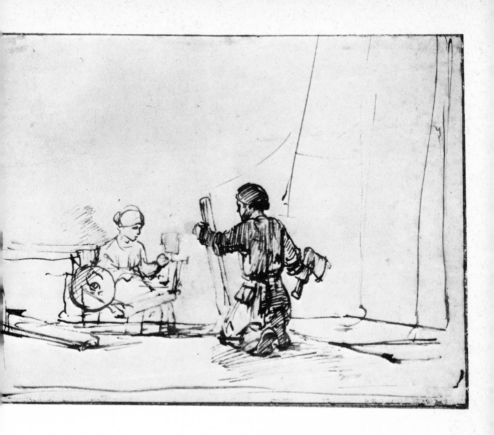

53
Landscape with a Stone Bridge, c. 1648-50

Pen and brush, brown ink, 133 x 219 mm
Louvre, Paris (B. 848). See p. 28

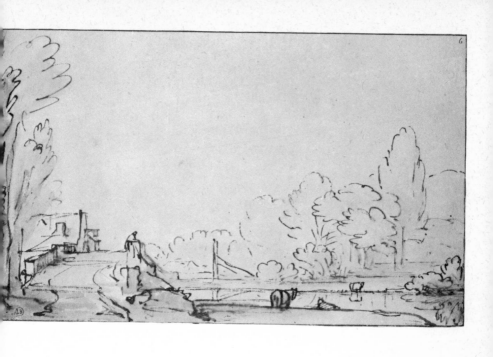

54
View Across the Amstel, 1648-50

Pen and brush, brown ink, on vellum, 132 x 232 mm
Rijksprentenkabinet, Amsterdam (B. 844)

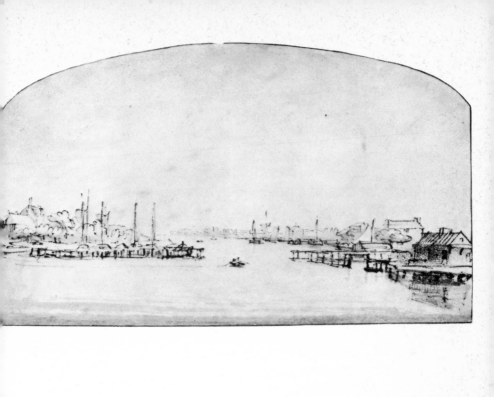

55
Winter Landscape, c. 1649-50

Pen and brush, brown ink, 67 x 161 mm
Fogg Art Museum, Cambridge, Massachusetts (B. 845)

56
View of Diemen, c. 1648-50

Pen and brush, brown ink, 112 x 175 mm
Private collection (B. 838)
Signed by a later hand: Rembrand

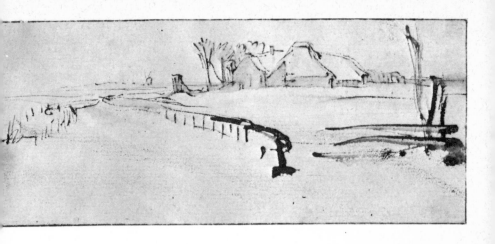

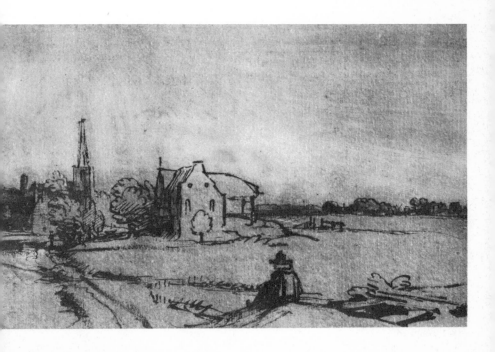

57
View Across the Nieuwe Meer near Amsterdam (?), c. 1649-50

Pen and brush, brown ink, 88 x 181 mm
Chatsworth Settlement (formerly the Duke of Devonshire Collection)

58
View of Diemen, c. 1649-50

Pen and brush, brown and gray ink, on brownish paper, 90 x 170 mm
Teylers Museum, Haarlem (B. 122)

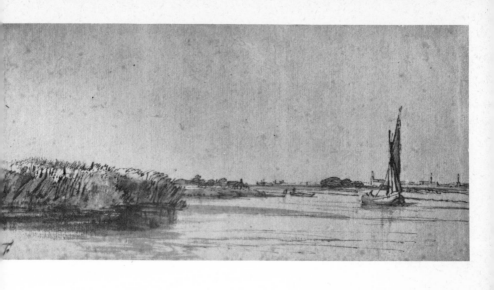

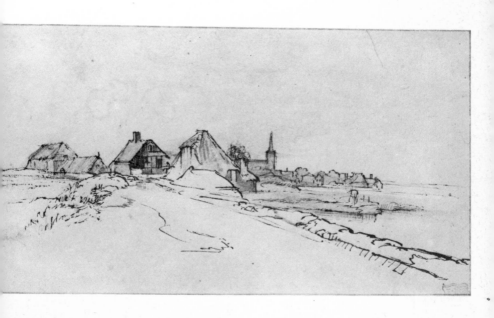

59
The Amstel Dike near Trompenburg, c. 1649-50

Pen and brush, brown ink, some white, on brown prepared paper, 130 x 217 mm
Chatsworth Settlement (B. 121)

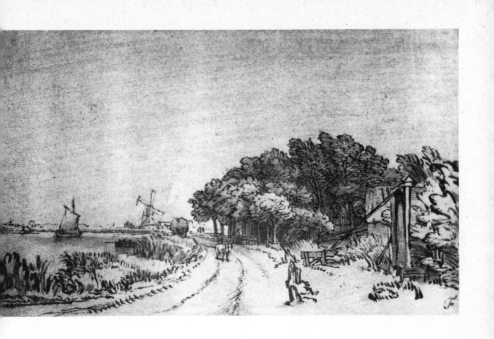

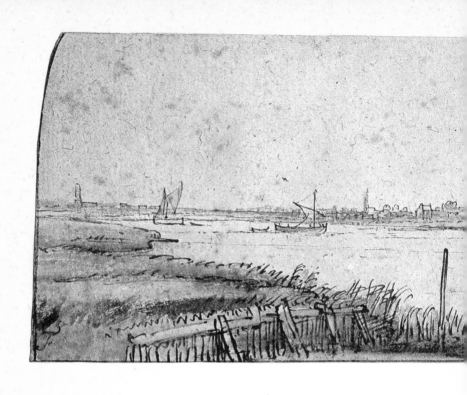

60

View Across the IJ from the Diemen Dike, c. 1649–50

Pen and brush, brown ink, some white, on grayish paper, 76 x 244 mm
Chatsworth Settlement (B. 123)

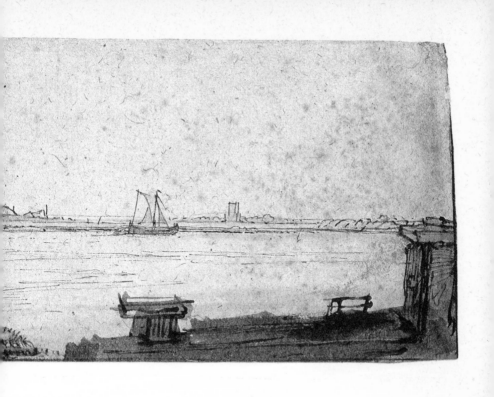

61

A Farmhouse Among Trees, c. 1650-51

Pen and brush, brown ink, on buff paper, 172 x 271 mm
Metropolitan Museum of Art, New York. H. O. Havemeyer Collection (B. 124)

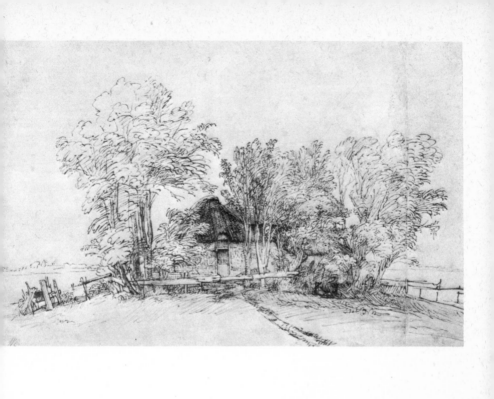

62
Landscape with the "Huys met het Toorentje," c. 1650-52

Pen and brush, brown ink, 98 x 218 mm
Collection Robert von Hirsch, Basel (B. 1267). See p. 28

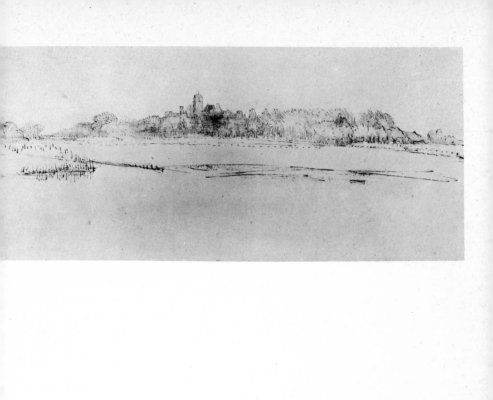

63

David Receiving the News of Uriah's Death, c. 1650-55

Pen, brown ink, some white, 195 x 290 mm
Rijksprentenkabinet, Amsterdam (B. 890)
Signed in two different later hands: Rembrand van Rhijn and Rembrandt van Rein

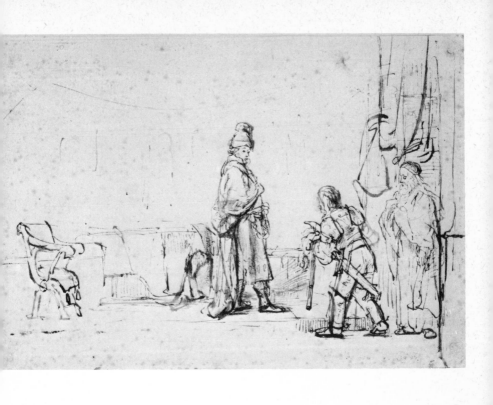

64

Mercury and Argus, c. 1651-52

Pen and brush, brown ink, corrected with white, 178 x 146 mm
Louvre, Paris (B. 884)

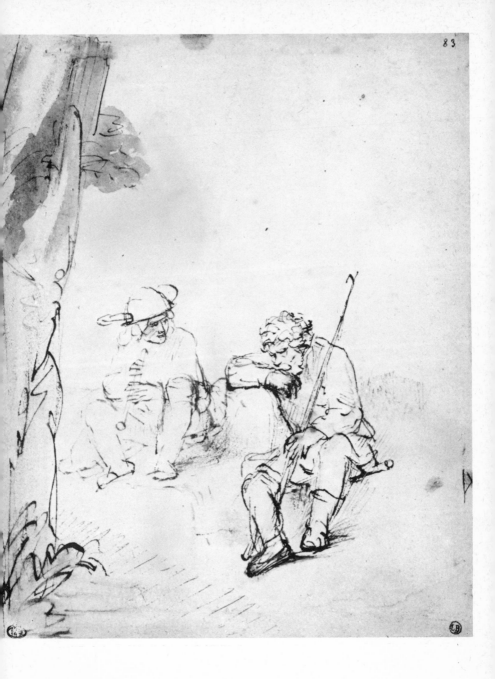

83

65

Homer Reciting His Verses, 1652

Pen, brown ink, 265 x 190 mm
Six Collection, Amsterdam (B. 913)
This drawing was made by Rembrandt in Jan Six's *Liber Amicorum*

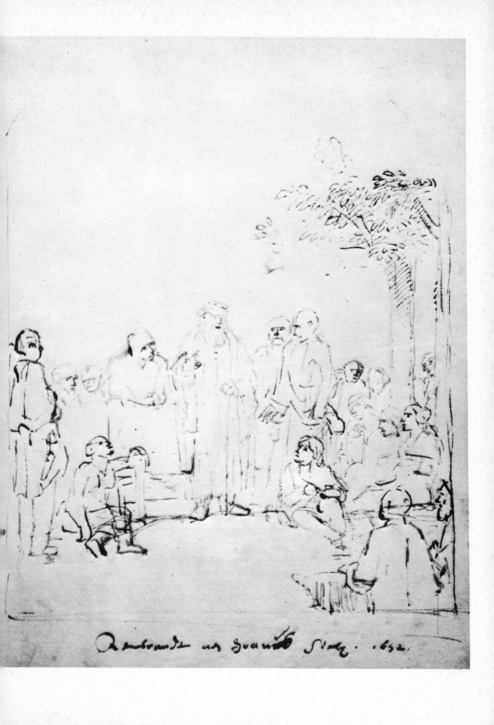

Rembrandt has zwaard Sidy. 1652.

66

The Ruins of the Old Town Hall, Amsterdam, After the Fire, 1652

Pen and brush, brown ink, touches of red chalk, 150 x 201 mm
Inscribed by Rembrandt: Vand waech afte sien Stats Huis van Amsteldam doent afgebrandt was den 9 Julij
1652. Rembrandt van rijn (As seen from the weigh-house, the Town Hall of Amsterdam after it was burned
down, July 9, 1652)
Rembrandthuis, Amsterdam (B. 1278). See p. 21

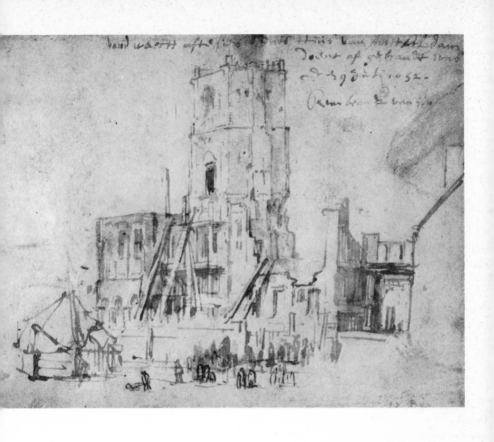

67

The Montelbaan Tower, Amsterdam, c. 1652-53

Pen and brush, brown ink, 145 x 144 mm
Rembrandthuis, Amsterdam (B. 1309). See p. 21
Signed by two different later hands: Rembrand and Rembrant

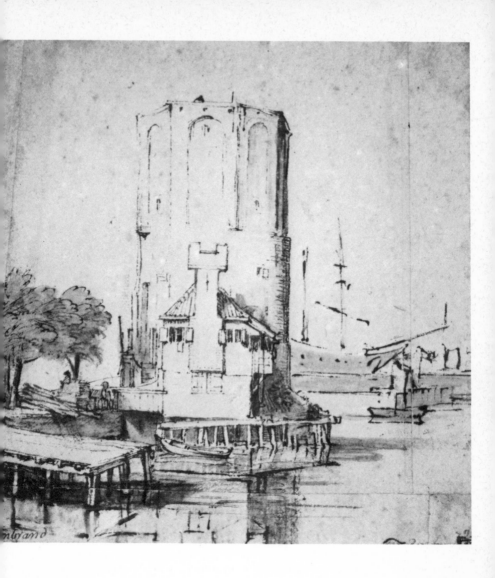

68

A Farmhouse and Trees, c. 1652-53

Pen and brush, brown ink, touches of white and red chalk, 108 x 178 mm
Nationalmuseum, Stockholm (B. 1292)
Signed by a later hand: Rimbrant

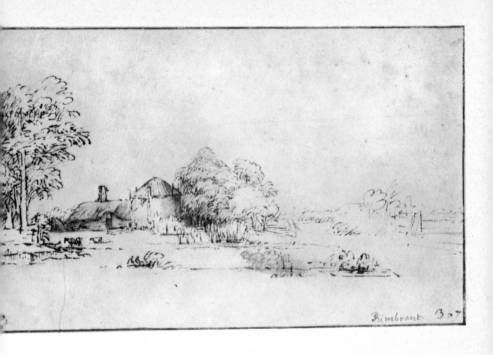

Rembrant. 307

69

The Holy Family, c. 1652

Pen and brush, brown ink, 220 x 191 mm
Albertina, Vienna (B. 888)

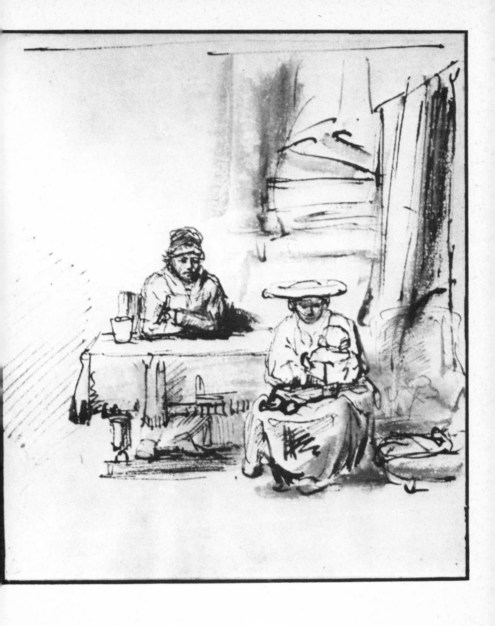

70

Lion Lying Down, c. 1652

Pen and brush, brown ink, heightened with white, on brownish paper, 140 x 203 mm
Museum Boymans-van Beuningen, Rotterdam (B. 1211). See p. 20

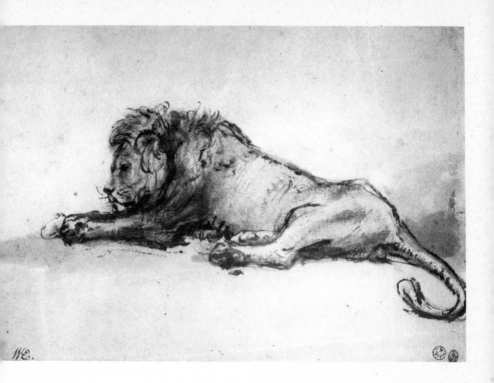

71

Daniel in the Lions' Den, c. 1652

Pen and brush, brown ink, touches of white and red chalk, 221 x 183 mm
Rijksprentenkabinet, Amsterdam (B. 887). See p. 20

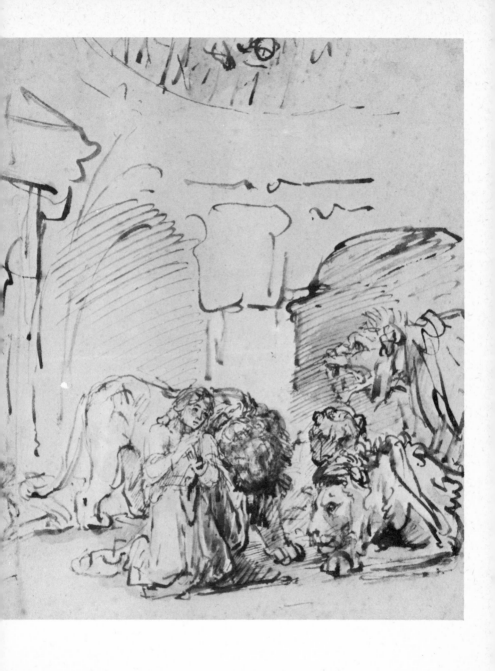

72

Christ Among the Doctors, c. 1652-54

Pen, brown ink, 188 x 225 mm
Nationalmuseum, Stockholm (B. 936)

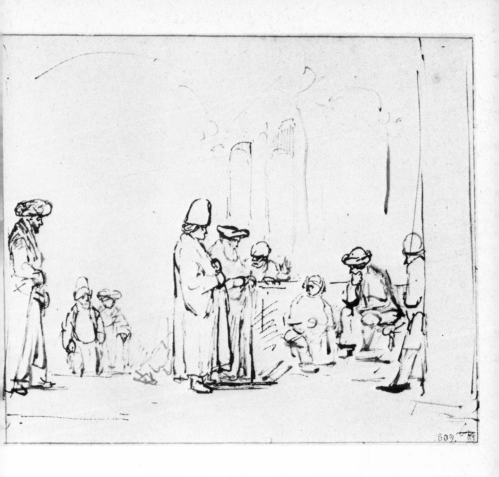

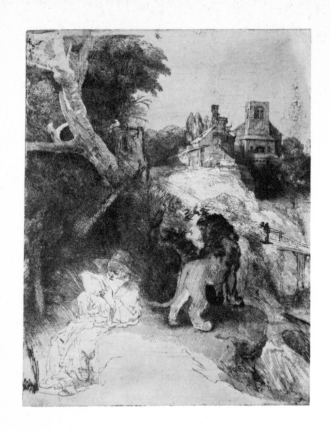

73a

St. Jerome Reading in a Landscape, c. 1653–54

Etching and burin, 259 x 210 mm (Ba. 104)

73

St. Jerome Reading in a Landscape, c. 1653–54

Study for plate 73a
Pen and brush, brown ink, 250 x 207 mm
Kunsthalle, Hamburg (B. 886)

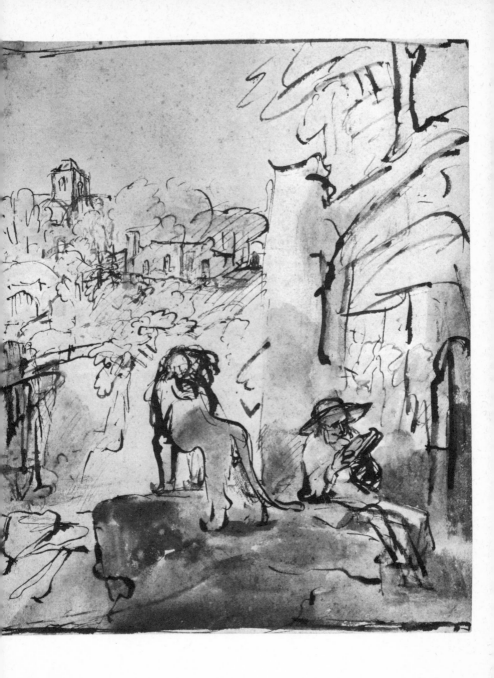

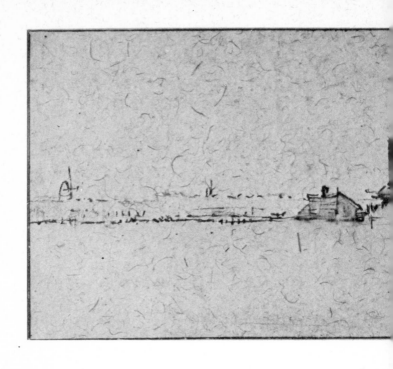

74

View Across the Amstel with the Inn "Het Molentje," c. 1654

Pen and brush, brown ink, some white, on roughly textured India paper, 82 x 226 mm
Fitzwilliam Museum, Cambridge (B. 1353). See p. 28

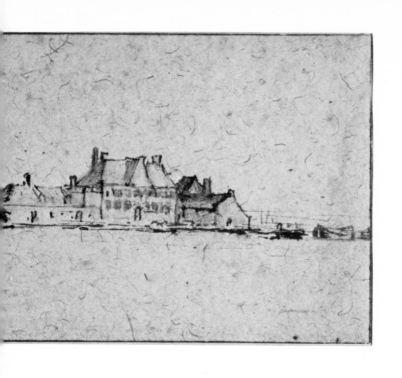

75

View of the Amstel with a Man Bathing, c. 1654-55

Pen and brush, brown ink, some white, 146 x 273 mm
Kupferstichkabinett, Staatliche Museen, Berlin-Dahlem (B. 1352)

76

Windmills to the West of Amsterdam, c. 1654-55

Pen and brush, brown ink, on gray paper, 120 x 263 mm
Kobberstiksamling, Copenhagen (B. 1335). See p. 28

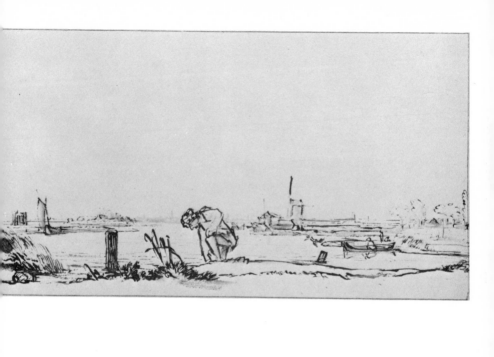

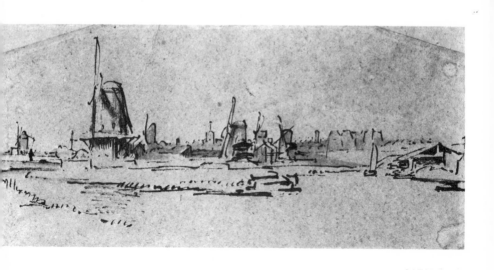

77

The Washing of the Feet, c. 1653-55

Pen, brown ink, 156 x 220 mm
Rijksprentenkabinet, Amsterdam (B. 931)

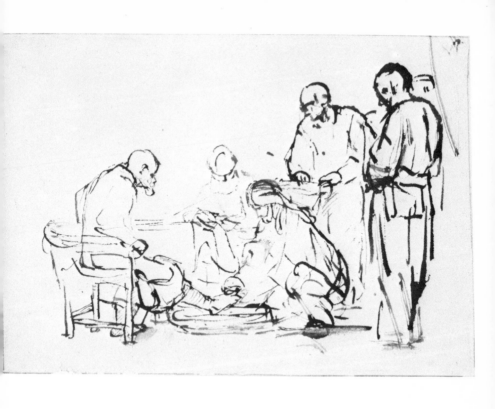

78

Christ in the Storm on the Sea of Galilee, c. 1654-55

Pen, brown ink, 197 x 300 mm
Kupferstichkabinett, Dresden (B. 954)

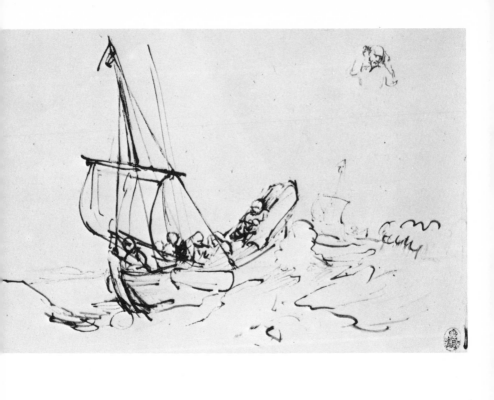

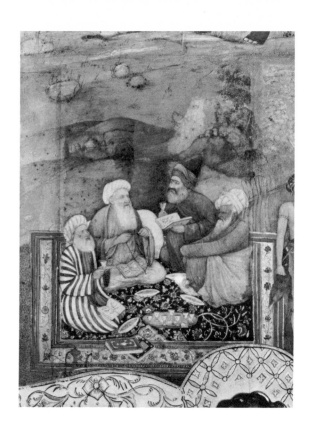

79a

Mogul Miniature (detail)

Schloss Schönbrunn, Vienna

79

Four Dervishes Seated Beneath a Tree, c. 1654-56

Pen and brush, brown ink, on Japanese paper, 194 x 125 mm
British Museum, London (B. 1187). See p. 18
Copy after the miniature

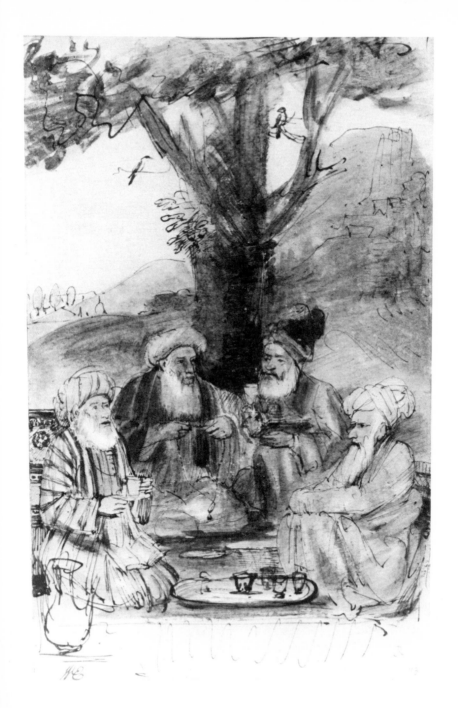

80

The Emperor Jahangir Receiving an Address, c. 1654-56

Pen and brush, brown ink, on Japanese paper, 210 x 183 mm
British Museum, London (B. 1190). See p. 18
Copy after a Mogul miniature

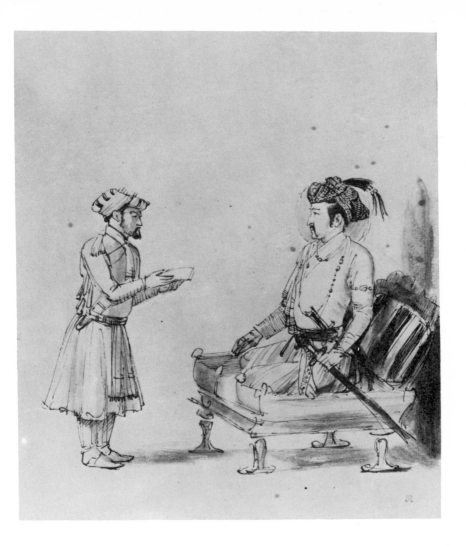

81

Self-Portrait, c. 1655-56

Pen, brown ink, on brownish paper, 203 x 134 mm
Rembrandthuis, Amsterdam (B. 1171). See p. 20
Inscription in 18th-century handwriting on the strip of paper attached below: getekent door Rembrant van
Rhijn naer sijn selves sooals hij in sijn schilderkamer gekleet was (Rembrandt van Rijn, drawn by himself, as
he used to dress in his studio)

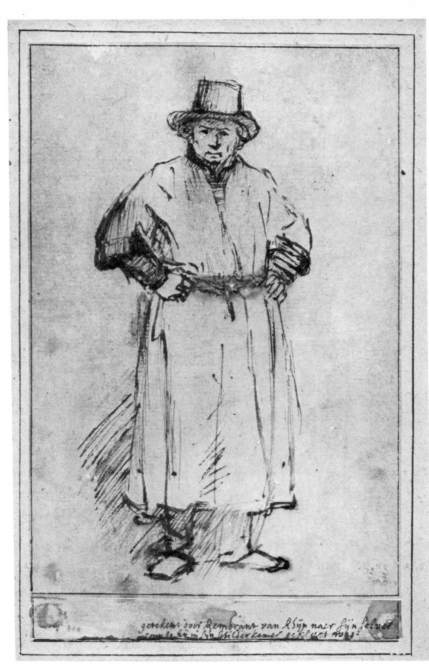

getekent door Rembrant van Rhijn naer sijn selver
van de ... in sijn Schilderkamer getelint 1655

The Skeleton Rider, c. 1655

Pen, brown ink, 157 x 154 mm
Hessisches Landesmuseum, Darmstadt (B. 728)

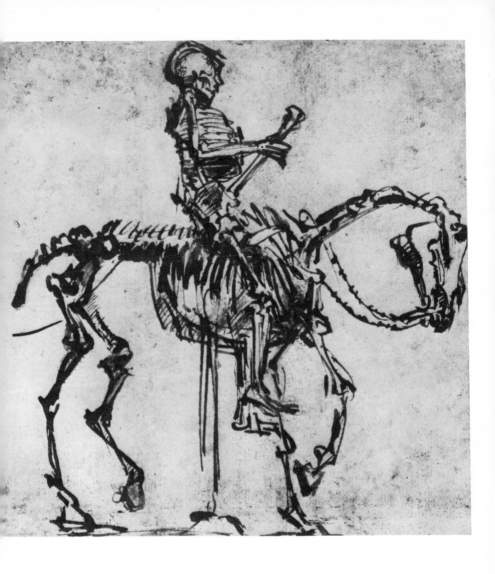

A Coach, c. 1655 (?)

Pen and brush, brown ink, 194 x 254 mm
British Museum, London (B. 756)

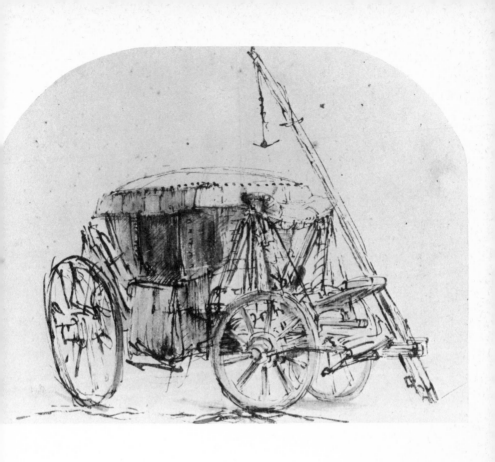

84

Woman Looking Out of a Window, c. 1655-56

Pen and brush, brown ink, 292 x 162 mm
Louvre, Paris (B. 1099)

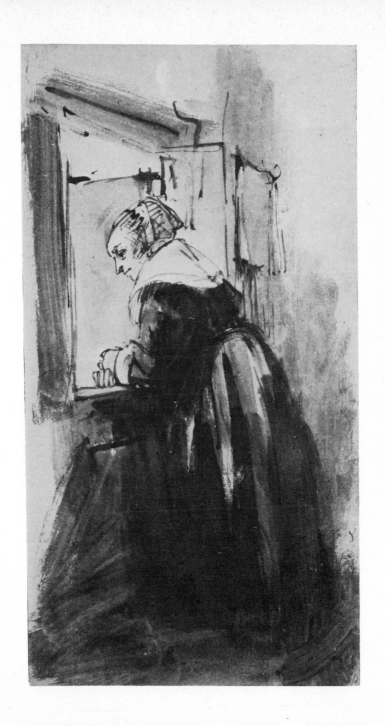

85

A Girl Sleeping, c. 1655-56

Brush, brown ink, 245 x 203 mm
British Museum, London (B. 1103)

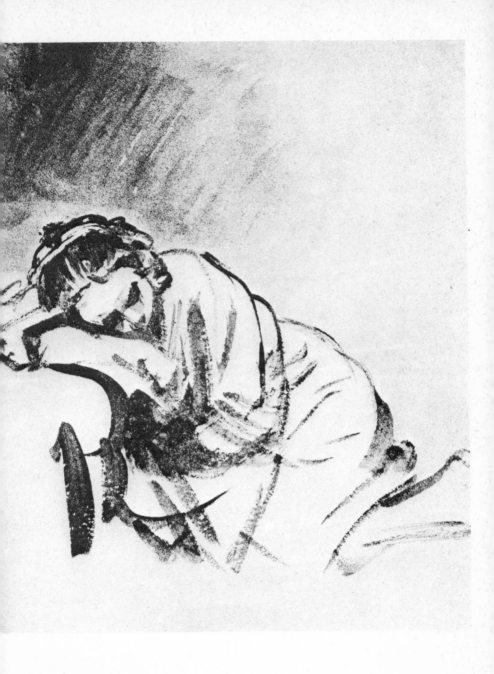

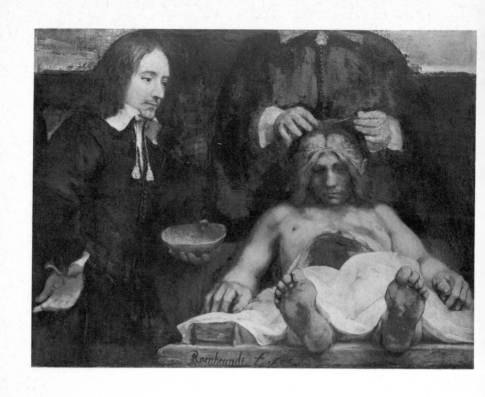

86a

The Anatomy Lesson of Dr. Joan Deyman (fragment), 1656

Canvas, 100 x 134 cm
Signed and dated
Rijksmuseum, Amsterdam, on loan from the city of Amsterdam (Br. 414)

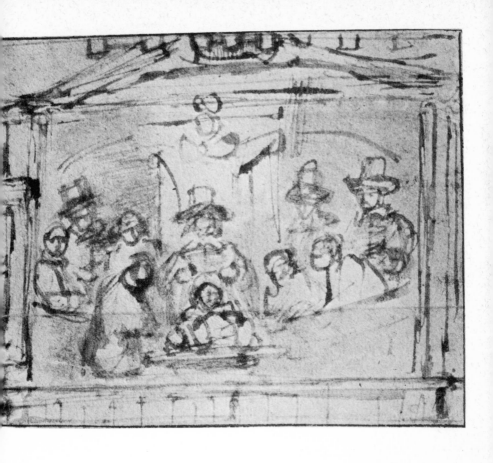

86

Sketch of "The Anatomy Lesson of Dr. Joan Deyman" with frame, 1656

Pen, brown ink, 110 x 133 mm
Rijksprentenkabinet, Amsterdam (B. 1175). See p. 17

87
Female Nude Asleep, c. 1657-58

Pen and brush, brown ink, 135 x 283 mm
Rijksprentenkabinet, Amsterdam (B. 1137). See p. 20

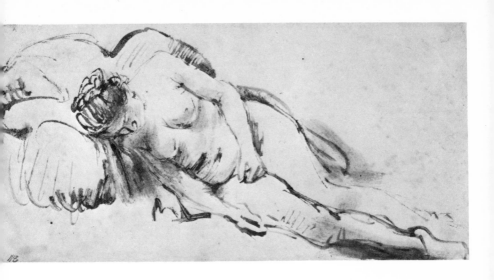

88

Cottages Among High Trees, c. 1657–58

Pen and brush, brown ink, 195 x 310 mm
Kupferstichkabinett, Staatliche Museen, Berlin-Dahlem (B. 1367)

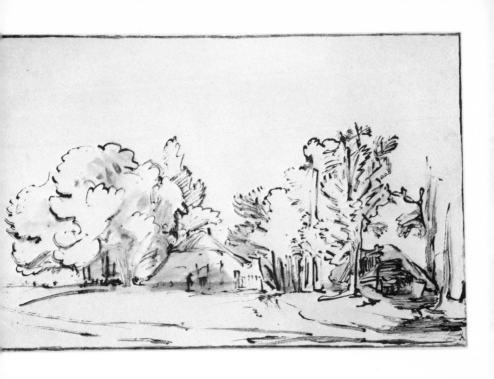

89

Christ and the Woman Taken in Adultery, c. 1659-60

Pen and brush, brown ink, some red and gray washes by a later hand, 170 x 202 mm
Inscription by Rembrandt on the strip of paper attached below: Soo jachtig om Christus in zijn antwoordt
te verschalken, kon de schrift... antw... niet afwachten (So eager to ensnare Christ in his own reply, the
scribes could not wait for the answer)
Staatliche Graphische Sammlung, Munich (B. 1047)

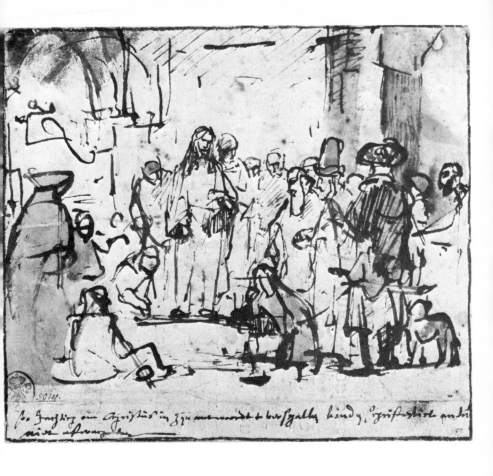

90

The Presentation in the Temple, 1661

Pen and brush, brown ink, heightened with white, 120 x 89 mm
Signed and dated: Rembrandt f. 1661
Royal Library, The Hague (B. 1057)
Drawing in the *Album Amicorum* of Dr. Jacobus Heyblock, minister and rector of the Gymnasium at Amsterdam

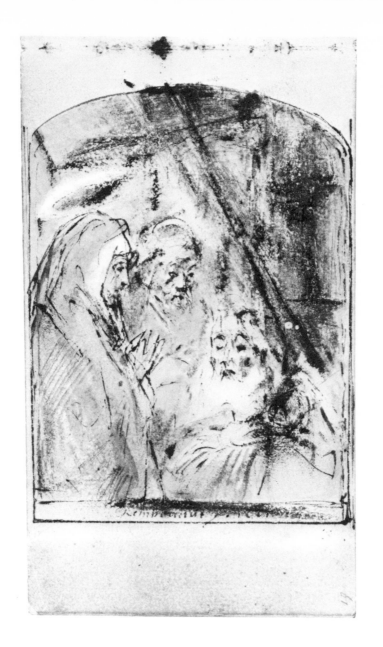

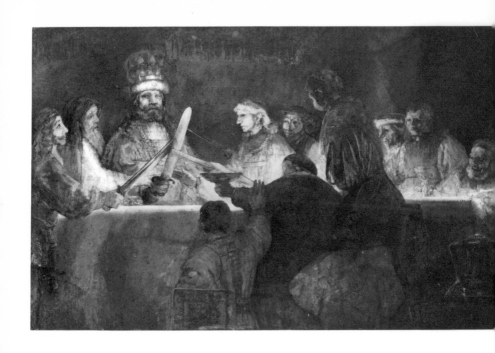

91a

The Conspiracy of the Batavians (fragment), c. 1661-62

Canvas, 196 x 309 cm
Nationalmuseum, Stockholm (Br. 482)

91

The Conspiracy of the Batavians, c. 1661

Study for plate 91a
Pen and brush, brown ink, some white, 196 x 180 mm, rounded at the top
Staatliche Graphische Sammlung, Munich (B. 1061). See pp. 17, 21
Drawn on the reverse of the announcement of the funeral of Rebecca de Vos, October 25, 1661

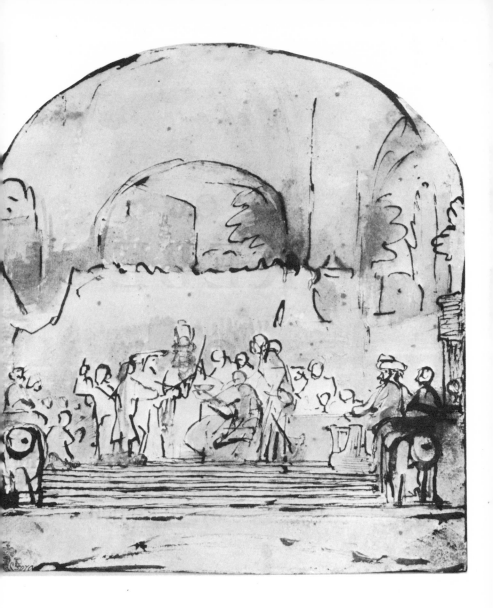

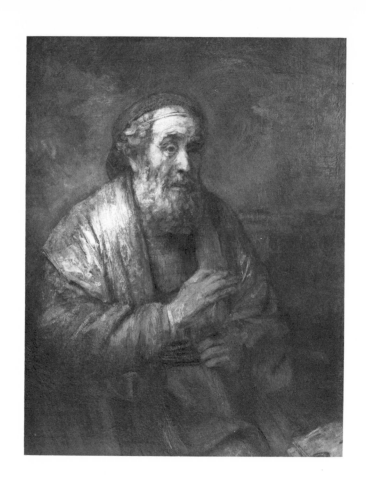

92a

Homer Dictating to a Scribe (fragment), 1663

Canvas, 108 x 82.5 cm
Signed and dated
Mauritshuis, The Hague (Br. 483)

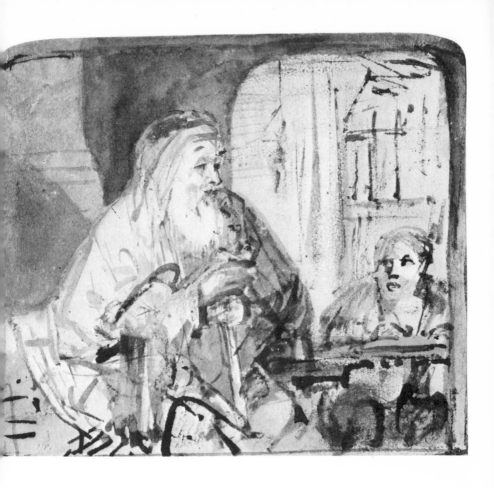

92

Homer Dictating to a Scribe, c. 1661–63

Study for plate 92a
Pen and brush, brown ink, heightened with white, gray and brown wash, partly by a later hand, 145 x 167 mm,
top corners rounded off
Nationalmuseum, Stockholm (B. 1066)

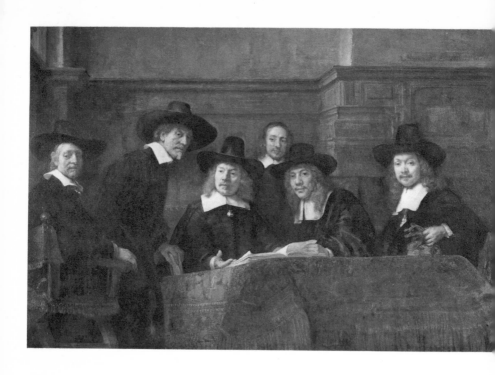

93a

The Sampling Officials of the Drapers' Guild, 1662

Canvas, 191 x 279 cm
Signed and dated
Rijksmuseum, Amsterdam, on loan from the city of Amsterdam (Br. 415)

93

Study for one of the Sampling Officials, c. 1662

Pen and brush, brown ink, corrected with white, 225 x 175 mm
Museum Boymans-van Beuningen, Rotterdam (B. 1180). See pp. 17, 21
Drawn on a sheet from a cashbook, the study probably represents Valckert Jansz.

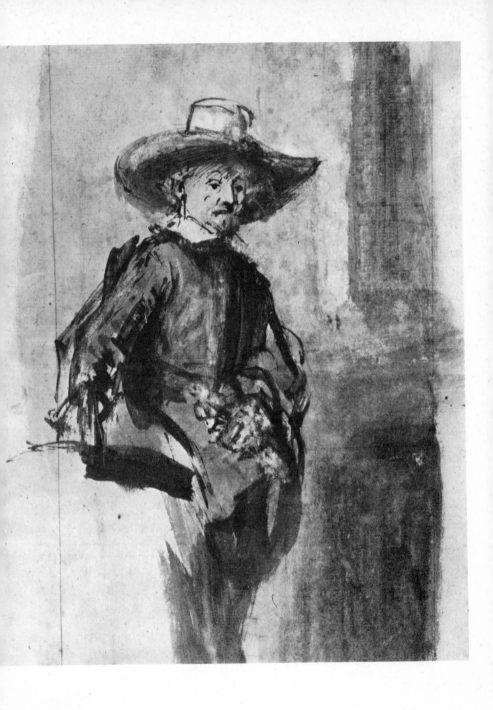

94
Diana and Actaeon, c. 1662-65

Pen and brush, brown ink, heightened with white, 246 x 347 mm
Kupferstichkabinett, Dresden (B. 1210). See p. 30
Signed by a later hand: Rembrant

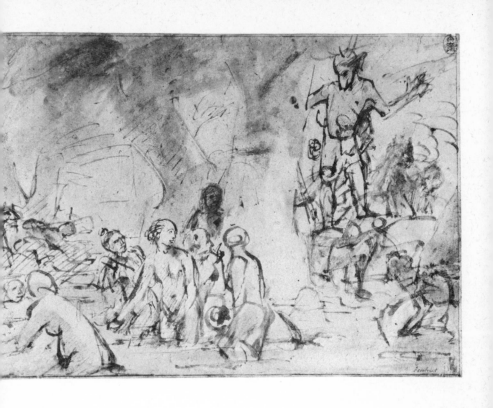

95

St. Peter at the Deathbed of Tabitha, c. 1662-63

Pen, brown ink, 190 x 273 mm
Kupferstichkabinett, Dresden (B. 1068). See p. 30

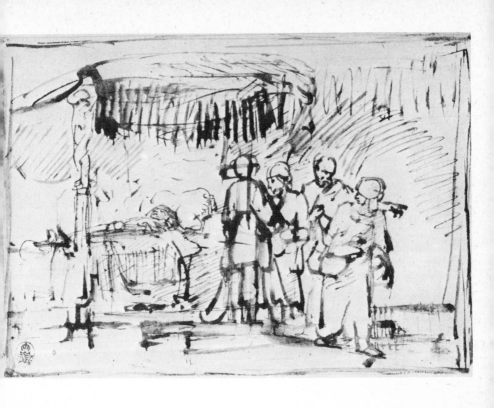

Selected Bibliography

Catalogues of Rembrandt's Work

Paintings

Hofstede de Groot, Cornelis. *A Catalogue Raisonné of the Works of the Most Eminent Dutch Painters of the Seventeenth Century,* based on the work of John Smith, translated by Edward G. Hawke, vol. VI: *Rembrandt and Maes.* London, 1916

Br.   Bredius, Abraham. *The Paintings of Rembrandt.* Phaidon Edition. New York: Oxford University Press, 1942

Bauch, Kurt. *Rembrandt Gemälde.* Berlin: Walter de Gruyter, 1966

Gerson, Horst. *Rembrandt's Paintings.* New York: Reynal & Company in association with William Morrow & Company, 1968

Drawings

Hofstede de Groot, Cornelis. *Die Handzeichnungen Rembrandts: Versuch eines beschreibenden und kritischen Katalogs.* Haarlem, 1906

B.   Benesch, Otto. *The Drawings of Rembrandt: A Critical and Chronological Catalogue.* 6 vols. London, New York: Phaidon Press, 1954-1957

Slive, Seymour. *Drawings of Rembrandt, with a Selection of Drawings by His Pupils and Followers.* 2 vols. New York: Dover Publications, 1965

Etchings

Ba.   Bartsch, Adam. *Catalogue raisonné de toutes les estampes qui forment l'oeuvre de Rembrandt et ceux de ses principaux imitateurs.* Vienna, 1797

Hind, Arthur M. *A Catalogue of Rembrandt's Etchings, Chronologically Arranged and Completely Illustrated.* 2 vols., 2nd ed. London: Methuen, 1923

Münz, Ludwig. *The Etchings of Rembrandt: Reproductions of the Whole Original Etched Work.* 2 vols. London: Phaidon Press, 1952

Biörklund, George, in association with O. H. Barnard. *Rembrandt's Etchings, True and False.* Stockholm, London, New York, 1955

Boon, K. G. *Rembrandt: The Complete Etchings.* New York: Harry N. Abrams, 1963

White, Christopher. *Rembrandt as an Etcher.* 2 vols. London, 1969

General Studies

Vosmaer, Carel. *Rembrandt Harmens van Rijn, sa vie et ses oeuvres.* The Hague: Martinus Nijhoff, 1868

Benesch, Otto. "Rembrandt Harmensz. van Rijn," in Ulrich Thieme and Felix Becker, *Allgemeines Lexikon der bildenden Künstler von der Antike bis zur Gegenwart,* vol. XXIX. Leipzig: Wilhelm Engelmann, 1935

Gelder, H. E. van. *Rembrandt.* 2nd rev. ed. Amsterdam: H. J. W. Becht, n.d. ("Palet" series)

Knuttel Wzn, G. *Rembrandt: De meester en zijn werk.* Amsterdam: Ploegsma, 1956

Rosenberg, Jakob. *Rembrandt: Life and Work.* Rev. ed. London, New York: Phaidon Press, 1964

White, Christopher. *Rembrandt and His World.* London: Thames and Hudson, 1964. See also the Dutch translation of this work, *Rembrandt, biografie in woord en beeld,* with additional notes by H. F. Wijnman. The Hague: Kruseman, 1964

Münz, Ludwig. *Rembrandt Harmenszoon van Rijn,* with additional commentaries by Bob Haak. Rev. ed. New York: Harry N. Abrams, 1967

Haak, Bob. *Rembrandt: His Life, His Work, His Time.* New York: Harry N. Abrams, 1969

5

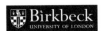